WHAM-O
SUPER·BOOK

WHAM-O

CELEBRATING 60 YEARS INSIDE THE FUN FACTORY!

SUPER·BOOK

TIM WALSH

CHRONICLE BOOKS
SAN FRANCISCO

Library of Congress Cataloging-in-Publication Data:

Walsh, Tim, 1964–
    Wham-O super-book : celebrating 60 years inside the fun factory /
    Tim Walsh.
       p. cm.
    Includes bibliographical references.
    ISBN 978-0-8118-6445-9
    1. Toys—History. 2. Games—History. 3. Wham-O, Inc. I. Title.

  GV1218.5.W35 2005
  688.72—dc22

                                              2008009916

Manufactured in China

Designed by Jacob Covey

10 9 8 7 6 5 4 3 2 1

Chronicle Books LLC
680 Second Street
San Francisco, CA 94107
www.chroniclebooks.com

Trademarks FRISBEE®, SLIP 'N SLIDE®, HULA HOOP®, and SUPERBALL® are registered trademarks of Wham-O Inc. All rights reserved. BUBBLE THING® is a registered trademark of David Stein. MYLAR® is a registered trademark of E. I. du Pont de Nemours and Company. THE OLYMPIC RINGS are a trademark of the International Olympic Committee. POWER WHEELS® is a registered trademark of Fisher-Price, a subsidiary of Mattel, Inc. ROLLER RACER® is a registered trademark of Mason Corporation. SCHWINN® is a registered trademark of Pacific Cycle, Inc. SILLY STRING® is a registered trademark licensed to Just For Kicks™ and owned by Julius Samann Ltd. All other trademarks are the property of their respective owners.

Photography Credits All product photographs were taken by Herb Booth of Booth Studio (www.boothstudio.com) unless otherwise noted. All period photographs, advertisements, sale sheets, product label images, and catalogs are from the WHAM-O company archives unless otherwise noted.
    Rich Knerr school portrait, p. 5; courtesy of South Pasadena High School. Arthur "Spud" Melin school portrait, p. 5; courtesy of Flintridge Preparatory School.
    Spud and Rich, p. 14; Knerr garage/shed, p. 16; Santa weapons ad, p. 35; Chain Gang Coasters, p. 51; Bowmatic, p. 57; Boomerang Saucer ad, p. 78; Circus Cycle, p. 96; Super Foam Machine, p. 147; Super-Looper, p. 147; SuperBall Baseball, p. 156; Fun Fountain, p. 168; Poke-a-Bone, p. 168; courtesy of Lori Knerr. Used with permission.
    Spud portrait, p. 20; Rich portrait, p. 21; Whirlo Way drawing, p. 74; Flyin-Saucer, p. 75; Pluto Platter, p. 76; Fred in space suit, p. 80; Rich, Fred,

and Spud, p. 82; Ed Headrick portrait, p. 89; courtesy of Phil Kennedy. Used with permission.
    John Stalberger, p. 45, courtesy of John Stalberger and the Footbag Hall of Fame. Used with permission.
    Boogie boarder, p. 179, courtesy of WHAM-O. Photograph by Maurice Aubuchon.
    Ashley Whippet, p. 85, courtesy of Tom Wehrli. Used with permission.
    Tom Wehrli and Murray, p. 88, courtesy of Tom Wehrli. Photo by Mark Pastor.
    John Begoske, p. 85, courtesy of the United States Guts Players Association. Photograph by Barb Thornton.
    Wheelie Bar, p. 97, from the collection of Devlin Thompson.
    Spud sliding, p. 20; Rich and Girl with Monster Bubbles, p. 21; Spud and Rich with secretary, p. 26; Norm Stingley sitting on SuperBall cartons, p. 158; © 2007 Polaris Communications. Photo by Lawrence Schiller. Used with permission.
    Weapons flyer, p. 30; Advertisements, p. 31; Tether Baseball ad, p. 38; Tether game, Floor Tennis, WHAM-IT, and Snowball ads, p. 39; Giant Tennis Bird, p. 40; Trac Ball box scan, p. 42; Hacky Patent, p. 47; Hula Hoop patent, p. 69; Frisbie Pie Company photograph, p. 80; Frisbee ad, p. 78; Wheelie Bar TV ad captures, p. 97; Double Auto Racer, p. 104; Bubble Thing test photograph, p. 117; Cricket House TV ad captures, p. 121; Monster Magnet TV ad captures, p. 127; Willie TV ad captures, p. 128; SuperElasticBubblePlastic TV ad captures, p. 151; Frisbee TV ad captures, p. 177; from the author's collection. Used with permission.

DEDICATED WITH ADMIRATION TO
ARTHUR "SPUD" MELIN (1925–2002) AND RICH KNERR (1925–2008)

Highest thanks to God. This is what the Lord Almighty says: "Once again men and women of ripe old age will sit in the streets of Jerusalem, each with cane in hand because of his age. The city streets will be filled with boys and girls playing there." (Zechariah 8:4–5)

Very special thanks to Sarah, Kate, and Emma. Your patience, encouragement, and love never cease to amaze me.

Special thanks to Lori Knerr. At every turn you helped by sharing your time, your collection, and most of all your passion and enthusiasm for your family's legacy.

Thanks to Richard Bebee, Mike Carrier, Kirk Demarais, Mojde Esfandiari, Marcia Fairbanks, Dan Goodsell, Chris Guirlinger, Gary Headrick, Phil Kennedy, Jason Liebig, Suzy Melin, Steve Mockus, Fred Morrison, Jim O'Donnell, Devlin Thompson, Dan Roddick, Michelle Gravino Royster, Laura Sciutti, Rick Shean, Miki Springsteen, John Stalberger, Norm Stingley, Steve Taylor, Barb Thornton, David Tolmer, and Tom Wehrli. You helped make this book better than it would have been without you.

Lastly, thanks to Rich Knerr. It meant a lot to me to get the chance to interview you for this book, and I very much wanted to hand you a finished copy with heartfelt appreciation. It wasn't meant to be. Thank you for giving me, and so many others, so much fun.

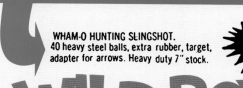

Water Fun

BACK OF THE COMIC BOOK

SUPER TOYS

WEIRDOS

COMPLETE WITH 45rpm RECORD, 2 STANDS, CROSS BAR

WHAT'S NEXT?

WHAM-O TIME LINE

BIBLIOGRAPHY

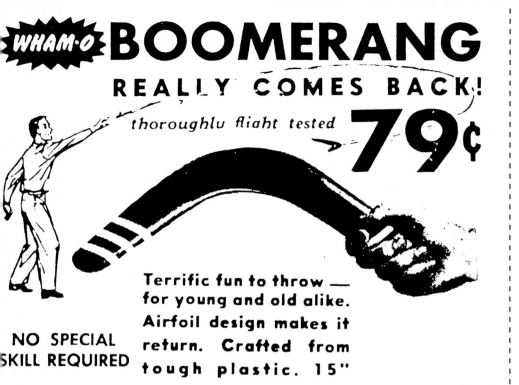

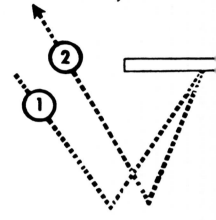
As a kid, I always had WHAM-O toys close at hand. At the epicenter of our household was the kitchen junk drawer filled with a hodgepodge of writing utensils, batteries, flashlights, nail clippers, a tube of SuperElasticBubblePlastic, and an assortment of SuperBalls. Yet this stuff was anything but junk. On the contrary, these were items that couldn't be "put away" for fear that they might be needed at a moment's notice. If I ever needed a little bounce in my step, SuperBall was there.

INTRODUCTION

Our garage held the larger WHAM-O playthings. There were assorted Frisbee discs, a Trac-Ball set, a water-stained Slip 'n Slide box, all at the ready. A Hula Hoop hung from the bicycle rack. The closet just off the garage contained wrapping paper, party supplies, and a can of Silly String. At any given moment, my brothers, sisters, and I were within a few feet of fun. The potential for play was palpable.

I discovered things while at play. I learned that a Frisbee could actually rise on a summer breeze and elevate my mood right along with it. I found out that the sticky mud and itchy grass plastered to my skin could be absolutely ignored if I happened to be standing in a neighborhood line of friends waiting for another trip down the Slip 'n Slide. And I learned, after discovering SuperBall's lethal second bounce the hard way (with a welt on my cheek to prove it), that playing with it thrilled me even more. There was something about its danger that enticed me to take my lumps and, like my favorite boyhood ball, bounce right back.

WHAM-O toys that I discovered for the first time in researching this book offered joyful revelation. I pushed my daughters on an old Roller Racer, and their squeals of delight attracted my wife, who also got a turn. We created the largest, most jaw-dropping bubbles any of us had ever seen with Bubble Thing. We laughed at Giant Comics and marveled at Magic Window. In the process, my wife and I learned something as simple as it is profound. Our kids are growing up too fast, and if we want to know what kind of young women they are becoming, there's no better way than through play.

Can you recall the first time you saw a Frisbee float in midair or saw someone spin a Hula Hoop in defiance of gravity? Ever see a group of kids giggle with glee while being chased by a Water Wiggle? Maybe an Air Blaster astonished you or a Wheelie-Bar made you stare in wonder. If a WHAM-O toy ever wowed you, then this is the book for you.

Rich Knerr and his lifelong friend and WHAM-O partner, Spud Melin, squeezed every drop of fun they could from life and it showed in all that they gave us. Their TV ads were fun. Their print ads were fun. Their hit toys were fun. Their fads, and even their flops, were fun. For sixty years the family culture they created has endured through the massive number of Hacky Sack and Frisbee fans who share a family bond.

Rich Knerr, his daughter Lori Knerr, and Spud's widow, Suzy Melin, have generously given me something that I have tried to pass on within these pages. After reading this book, it's my hope that you too will feel welcomed into the WHAM-O family.

—TIM WALSH

1

It's new··· It's different··

WILD BOYS

Richard P. Knerr and Arthur K. "Spud" Melin met through a mutual friend around 1942. "Spud was already in high school and I was just getting started," Rich said. "We were friends from the time we were teenagers." The boys graduated from high school and enrolled in the University of Southern California, but their minds were always on business instead of books. "We started selling things before I graduated, but Spud quit because he never really wanted to stay. He wasn't interested in school stuff. Besides, he was smarter than most of those guys there anyway."

PAGE 14: Ever the sportsmen, Rich and Spud would often go to Mexico for deep-sea fishing. Here they pose with their catches sometime in the early 1950s.

BELOW (LEFT AND RIGHT): This shed, attached to Rich Knerr's parents' garage on Le Droit Drive in South Pasadena, was where Rich and Spud made their first slingshot in 1948. The redwood workbench where the men cut and sanded their WHAM-O slingshots is still standing after sixty years.

Rich and Spud's ambition showed early. They first started an import-export business dealing in lumber. When that didn't turn out well, they sold used cars for a brief time. By the time Sports Motors sold its last car, Rich had earned a degree in business, but the two weren't all work. In 1948, having a mutual interest in falconry, they bought some birds. "We got a couple of young falcons and started training them," Rich recalled. "We had hawks too, but not for sale, just for fun." To teach the birds how to dive for prey, the hobbyists used a homemade slingshot to shoot meat into the air and unwittingly launched a business along with the meatballs.

In a story that is now legend, a man approached and inquired about buying a slingshot like the one they had made. The chance encounter lit their collective lightbulbs, and Rich and Spud found themselves, that day in 1948, very much back in business. "We bought a band saw from Sears & Roebuck for $7 down and $7 a month and set up shop in my mom and dad's garage," Rich said. "I cut out slingshots from good Southern ash, and Spud sanded them. We cut the straps out of pure gum rubber sheets from South America. We'd tie leather pouches on them, and that was it."

In Marvin Kaye's book, *A Toy Is Born*, the author quotes Rich as saying, ". . . we needed a name for our company. We thought of Fling-O, but that didn't seem to

have as much impact as Wham-O. *That* was the word for our slingshots." Thus the comic book sound of a slingshot projectile hitting its target inspired the naming of the WHAM-O Manufacturing Company. "We were all mail order in the beginning," Rich recalled. "In fact, that kept us financed. We ran ads and sold a lot of them."

With some success, the entrepreneurs moved out of the shed and into a place of their own. "There was an empty store down in Alhambra," Rich said. "We rented it and started to make other things. We were only there about two years before we got a factory in San Gabriel [California]." They would soon expand into weapons before going into sporting goods. "From the beginning, we looked for unique items that we thought would sell," Rich said. "Golly, we did throwing knives, blowguns, and crossbows because they were different. You couldn't buy those things just anywhere" (see chapter two, "Weapons").

It was years before WHAM-O left mail order behind and began mass production of its products. "There was no *mass* in our production in the early days," according to Rich. "We eventually got some sales reps onboard, and they hit the road. Sporting goods stores were the first to buy. Woolworth's and Sears were next. They were quite supportive." WHAM-O's first big hits were Hula Hoop and Frisbee, which allowed

BELOW: Rich and Spud sold their sole product by running ads like this one in *Popular Mechanics, Popular Science,* and *Field & Stream.*

Rich and Spud to grow their factory in San Gabriel, but even then they stayed lean, especially after Hula Hoop almost put them out of business. "After Hula Hoop, when we'd get an idea for a product, we'd hire the production of it out," Rich said. "We didn't want a whole bunch of money in machinery to build a product if we didn't know it would sell." This philosophy led to some peculiar products. With nothing to lose, the two entrepreneurs felt free to try just about anything (see chapter four, "Why Not?").

According to author Kaye of *A Toy Is Born*, ". . . by 1950, WHAM-O was moving into the toy and novelty area with cap guns and pellet guns, as well as navel stoles of genuine mink 'for the woman who has everything.'" Although you'll find quotes from my interviews with him scattered throughout this book, the following exchange with Rich Knerr is by far my favorite. It gives you a glimpse of the wit and humor this 82-year-old kid possessed and the love and admiration he had for his partner.

"Rich, what's a mink navel stole?" I asked.

[*Laughing*] "That was Spud's idea. [*lowering voice to imitate an announcer*] 'A Mink Navel Stole.'"

"What was it?"

ABOVE: Arthur "Spud" Melin. "He was a very well-balanced guy," Rich said of his lifelong friend. "He was smart, but really funny. He just had what it took to be somebody."

CENTER (LEFT AND RIGHT): In these never-before-published photos from a *Life* magazine shoot, Spud slips and slides (with a cigar!) and Rich plays with a little kid and WHAM-O's Giant Monster Bubbles.

"I guess it's popular now, but back then, women couldn't show their belly buttons. So the idea was to cover it up with a [*lowering voice again*] Mink Navel Stole."

"Was it like a mink belt?"

"No, it was like a paste-on. It was about the size of a quarter, just enough to cover up the belly button."

"So it was just a mink patch?"

"Yeah, that's right." [*Laughing*]

"How did *that* go over?"

"Oh, God. [*Long pause*] It was too early for its time. That was Spud. He was crazy. I had the greatest partner in the world. He was just a great guy."

Another idea of Spud's was the strange Mr. Hootie Rake, a miniature rake that was used to take the little white stringy thing off an egg yolk. "Spud was the quiet one, but he had a unique sense of humor," Frisbee inventor Fred Morrison said. "I know the Hootie Rake very well. I never saw one, but I heard all the conversations over there [at Wham-O] around it. It came with a carrying case you could wear on your belt." Spud's widow, Suzy Melin remembers the Mr. Hootie Rake as well. "Oh my gosh, do I? I still have one!" she gushed. "That was just Spud. He was a fun-loving man. Friends of our daughter would come over, knock on the door, and ask her, 'Can your Dad come out and play?' Sure enough, he'd go outside and play. 'Course he always had something that he wanted to try out on them."

Spud Melin died in 2002, at the age of 77. "Spud was a great man," Rich's daughter, Lori Knerr, said. "He had this wonderful smile and was so fun-loving. He had fun no matter what he was doing. Whenever we'd visit Dad at WHAM-O, we'd go right in to see Spud, because there was always something fun going on in his office. We all miss him."

"We were the closest friends. I never had a better one than that one," Rich shared. I asked Rich why he and Spud got along so well. "I don't know," he answered. "He was a poor judge of people, I guess."

Rich Knerr is larger than life. In almost every picture of him he has an ear-to-ear smile. It helps to have a childlike enthusiasm for your work when you play for a living. "We're always seeking what we call 'the magical degree of amazement' in our products," Rich said in a 1966 article from *Popular Science*. "We want people to exclaim, 'What was that?' or 'Gee, I never saw anything like that before.'" Frisbee inventor Fred Morrison witnessed something he'd never seen before when Rich and Spud's boyish mischief surfaced in 1965, the year SuperBall was released. "I'd never seen the damn things before and I didn't know what they were," Morrison recalled. "I was following their car down the freeway. All of the sudden here comes all these little black things bouncing all over hell, all over my car, all over the freeway. Here they're throwing these Mini SuperBalls out of the back of their car down the freeway! Their senses of humor were just something to be around."

WHAM-O

wamo MANUFACTURING COMPANY, 835 E. EL MONTE STREET SAN GABRIEL, CALIFORNIA

BIG BIRD

WHAM-O **PLUTO-PLATTER**

FLYING SAUCER
REALLY FLIES
sail them straight or in a curve 79¢
— BOOMERANGS !

#132

UNBREAKABLE! SOFT-SAFE

A FLICK OF THE WRIST—and your saucer sails away, up to 200 feet. Will fly straight, curve right or left, or return to you depending upon the angle you throw it. You can even play catch around a tree! Scientific airfoil causes lift—spinning gives stability in flight. Made of unbreakable polyethylene.

achieve skill with practice

SKIPS tilt at 45° angle, throw into ground

USE A BACKHAND flick of the wrist

Saucer bounces off into level flight

BOOMERANG tilt and throw upward

SKILL GAME play for points

PLAY CATCH-THROW CURVES when tilted slightly

FLYING SAUCER
HORSESHOE GAME

#132-A

$4.98 RETAIL

EACH PLAYER (OR SIDE) THROWS TWO DISCS. WHEN FOUR PEOPLE PLAY, EACH THROWS ONE DISC. DISC CLOSEST TO THE POST COUNTS ONE POINT. IF DISC HITS POST, THREE POINTS. IF LEANING AGAINST THE POST, FIVE POINTS. THE PLAYER WHOSE DISC IS FARTHEST FROM THE POST SUBTRACTS ONE POINT FROM HIS SCORE. TEN POINTS IS GAME.

WILLIE

WHAM-O # PADDLE TETHER BALL SET
$5.95 retail
#118

---fun for the entire family

Hilarious fun! Competitive sport! Skill game for all ages. Wonderful exercise— swell for parties. Set up anywhere in your yard. Opponents bat ball in opposite directions. You win by hitting ball past other player until it winds completely up to the pole. The game is wild but tames the kids. Includes 2 wooden paddles, cotton cord, ball, and 2-piece pole with connector, heavy duty.

Individually boxed

WATER WIGGLE

WHAM-O ®

MONSTER MAGNET

FRISBEE

965

OAST TO COAST

TV

ATURATION

SCHEDULE
PROMOTED IN OVER

100

MAJOR TV MARKETS
ON TOP-RATED ADVENTURE, CHILDREN'S AND DANCE PARTY SHOWS

AIR BLASTER

SLIP 'N SLIDE

WHA
SPOR
GOO
19

WHAM-O

Another fun factor that played into the unique atmosphere at WHAM-O was the fact that Rich and Spud were co-vice presidents of the company. There was no boss. "We were partners. We never really had any big disagreements. We agreed on most everything or we didn't do it," Rich said. Suzy Melin witnessed firsthand the unique relationship the two men shared. "Rich and Spud really needed each other to get that thing started. Each had his own gift. Rich was great with people and was very jolly and enthusiastic. That was his gift, in the sales area. Spud was more R&D. He was the idea man. He had this fabulous imagination and an innate good business sense."

Jenny Martinez, who started working for Rich and Spud in 1958 (and was still working for them when they sold their company in 1982), noted what made WHAM-O a family. "These two guys had been together since they were young. They were like brothers, so WHAM-O was more like a family than a company. It was the best place to work. They rented a bus once and took all of us out to Disneyland. Another time we all went to a Frisbee tournament in Pasadena. They were just very family oriented."

The line between the factory and the family was further blurred whenever Rich took new toy ideas home to his kids. "My dad was always bringing toys home for my sister, brother, and me to test," Lori Knerr recalled. "We were WHAM-O's R&D department! I remember he never told us what the toy was or what we were supposed to do with it. I guess he thought that if kids didn't get it, then they'd never get it, you know? He wanted to know what we thought."

As you'll learn in the following chapters, the family philosophy that Rich and Spud cultivated within WHAM-O would be imparted to two of their most famous products and connect people like few toys ever have. Frisbee fans and Hacky Sack fans are groups who don't just play the sports that have developed around their favorite WHAM-O playthings—they live them. And in doing so, they connect with others within a social network of play that is nothing short of family.

When a toy company makes some of the most identifiable toys in the world and sells those toys for thirty or forty years, another interesting family phenomenon happens: a second or even third generation of play. Toys connect us. When you set up a Slip 'n Slide for your child, you give him or her a shared experience. You played with one in your backyard when you were 10 years old. Passing on the love of your favorite boyhood ball and warning your nephew of SuperBall's deadly second bounce or teaching your daughter how to keep her Hula Hoop spinning in that gravity-defying manner are ways that WHAM-O has transcended generations of families.

Could Rich and Spud ever have predicted what their little slingshot shop would spawn? Could they have known that they'd survive the roller-coaster ride of the toy and novelty business and fads in play that come and go, like the Hula Hoop? A 1965 article from the *Wall Street Journal* reveals that WHAM-O earned roughly $370,000 in 1962, lost $425,000 in 1964, and earned $385,000 in 1965. "Such dependence on fads makes Wham-O anything but a stable company . . .," the article warned. Yet Rich

BELOW: In the early days, Rich and Spud relied on their intuition and a unique idea of market-testing by mail order. "We'd get an idea for something, make up an ad, and see if anybody wanted it," Rich explained. "If they ordered it, great, but if nothing happened, then that was the end of that."

believed. In the same piece, he is quoted as saying, "We're always out for what's new and different. We sit around and try to figure out what toys will stimulate imaginations in the year 2500. That just has to be something amazing."

What was truly amazing, as you will see repeatedly throughout this book, was Rich and Spud's willingness to try anything and their keen eye for finding what was "next." They understood that a hit plaything could come from anywhere—most likely from outside the walls of WHAM-O. Then, once a plaything was given that famous red starburst logo, Rich and Spud knew how to market it masterfully. Above all else, they knew that their greatest asset was the very thing they were creating, selling, and promoting . . . fun.

OPPOSITE: "*Life* did several stories on us," Rich recalled. "That was fun, and good for business." In this shot from 1965, Spud and Rich ham it up with a "secretary." "Anytime we'd bring out something new, they'd throw it in the magazine," he said. "And it was the biggest magazine out there. They were very good to us."

2

WEAPONS

Smashing Power!

It was a different time, but there's something very politically incorrect about WHAM-O's weapons era. So many sharp points and projectiles. "You'll put your eye out with that thing . . . and *that* thing . . . and *that* thing, too!" my mother would say. She'd be shocked and dismayed at the sight of the Powermaster Crossbow and the B.B. Gun. But so is anyone familiar only with the Hula Hoop era of the company history.

No, *this* WHAM-O was for grown-ups. That Jungle Machete with the "razor sharp" 2-foot blade? The one "used by natives in clearing trails and in hand-to-hand fighting"? Definitely not for kids. Still, I wonder . . . did grown men really hunt squirrels with an Apache Throwing Tomahawk? Were adults clamoring for WHAM-O's Malayan Throwing Dagger? WHAM-O weapons were aimed directly at their target audience: teenage boys.

All this weaponry reflected the interests of WHAM-O's founders. "We made weapons because we were inclined that way," Rich Knerr said. "We did blowguns and everything!" His excitement is evident from all the blowguns WHAM-O made. He and Spud really liked blowguns. There was the standard Malayan Blowgun, the Rifle Blowgun, the Borneo Hunting Blowgun, and even the Huf N'Puf Safe Blowgun, which shot rubber-tipped, suction-cup darts.

If teens and families were in the crosshairs of the early WHAM-O marketing machine, then it would be a natural progression for the company to move toward sports and games. Yet when the company introduced its Dart Game, it was obvious

MALAYAN
THROWING DAGGER
---- **BALANCED TO STICK** ----

#102

only $1.98 postpaid

This **MALAYAN FIGHTING KNIFE** is used for self-defense, killing game, target skill. A powerful, silent, accurate weapon. Splits 1" board at 30 ft.

Balanced to stick!

Fun, Thrills, Excitement! Indoors – outdoors. Learn this Sport! Easy to throw accurately with our clear instructions. Beautiful, heavy-duty 10" knife. Tempered steel. Tough, rawhide-bound handle. Rare souvenir, unusual bargain. Limited quantity. Sold direct only.

Check #102 on Handy Order Coupon

- *Exciting Sport!*
- *Easy to Learn!*
- *Fun-Indoors, Outdoors!*

Hunters!
This New Weapon Will Amaze You

#108

BORNEO HUNTING BLOWGUN

Most accurate native weapon ever devised! For killing game – self-defense – target skill. Silent and very powerful. **GUARANTEED TO GO THROUGH ¼" PLYWOOD!** Kills without poison. Darts go right through rabbits, squirrels, etc.

5 Foot Long Heavy Duty Hunting Model

Extra darts 6 for $1

$4.98 Postpaid

This is an amazing weapon. American sportsmen who first try it cannot believe their eyes — so accurate and powerful is this blowgun. Average person can hit a 2" bullseye at 30 ft. almost every time. Shoots over 300 ft. Precision made – ½" bore. Blue steel. Beautiful finish. Comes with six 5" steel hunting darts, target, instructions. Limited quantity.

A real precision instrument
Guaranteed Satisfaction or Money Refunded

Check #108 on Handy Order Coupon

Sportsmen!
Here is the Newest Target Sport
Fun -- Skill -- Action

#109

Apache THROWING TOMAHAWK
Balanced to stick

An ancient Indian weapon for killing game – target sport. Easy to throw with our clear instructions. Splits a 2" board at 30'. **Will stick from any angle**

$2.98 post paid

Rare Souvenir! Beautiful heavy duty 14" tomahawk. Solid tempered steel. Unusual bargain, limited supply. Sold direct only.

Anyone can quickly learn to throw it
Check #109 on Handy Order Coupon

that the transition would not be an easy one. A 1950 ad for the game reads like a Jekyll & Hyde copywriter's struggle to position the new sport/game somewhere between DEADLY and *delightful*.

SHOOT HORNET DARTS AND LISTEN TO THEM SING **WHAM-O.** *Your family and friends will have the time of their lives playing this newest game.* IT'S A REAL MAN'S GAME *and safe too. This easy pulling* SLINGSHOT SHOOTS HORNET DARTS *of soft rubber suction cups at a* SPECIALLY PROCESSED PLASTIC TARGET AT MORE THAN **100** MPH. *Target is colorful and the dart tails are bright red and blue plastic for easy scoring. For indoor* AND OUTDOOR USE — *it is ideal for the recreation room, den, or basement, and is guaranteed to be the life of the party.*

The WHAM-O Dart Game was followed by Jai-Alai and the Golfer's Home Practice Range. Mothers everywhere celebrated. While WHAM-O began as a company strictly for the sportsman, it now welcomed in a wider audience—the sports fan.

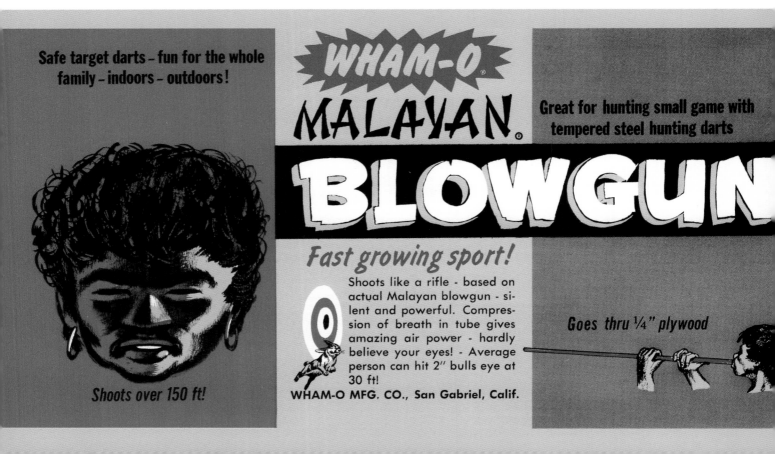

Safe target darts - fun for the whole family - indoors - outdoors!

Shoots over 150 ft!

WHAM-O

MALAYAN

BLOWGUN

Great for hunting small game with tempered steel hunting darts

Fast growing sport!

Shoots like a rifle - based on actual Malayan blowgun - silent and powerful. Compression of breath in tube gives amazing air power - hardly believe your eyes! - Average person can hit 2" bulls eye at 30 ft!

WHAM-O MFG. CO., San Gabriel, Calif.

Goes thru ¼" plywood

hufn'puf

REAL AFRICAN FAMILY FUN!

SAFE BLOWGUN

SHOOTS SOFT SAFE RUBBER DARTS
SUCTION CUPS • NO POINTS

SKILL GAME FOR ALL AGES

Watch the special darts zing to the

PLASTIC COATED TARGET

SPLAT!... A BULLSEYE!

Only 98¢

#185 ———— 1 DOZ. TO PKG.

PACKAGE CONTAINS BLOWGUN, FOUR RUBBER DARTS, PLASTIC COATED TARGET

WHAM-O MANUFACTURING COMPANY
835 E. El Monte Street, San Gabriel, California

WHAM-O FENCING SWORDS

These handsome swords have blades of
fine carbon spring steel and are ideal
for learning the art of
fencing.

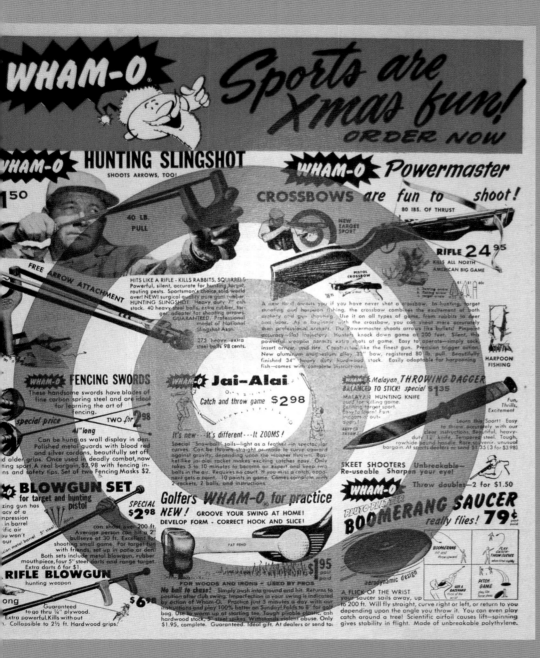

3

New GIANT

SPORTS

SKILL GAME —
KEEP SCORE

Since Rich Knerr and Spud Melin sold their hunting and target weapons mostly to sporting goods stores, it made sense that they would look to expand their line with "sports" as opposed to toys. Ads for WHAM-O's early sporting goods encouraged young adults to "hit it," "throw it," "sling it," "whack it," and even "WHAM-IT!" An early focus was on sports training devices and fitness equipment. Then in 1957 they struck gold with the Frisbee and shrewdly marketed it as a sport. In the search for another hit, WHAM-O produced many watered-down versions of already existing sports. It wasn't until they got original again that several sporting giants were born.

Only $1.75

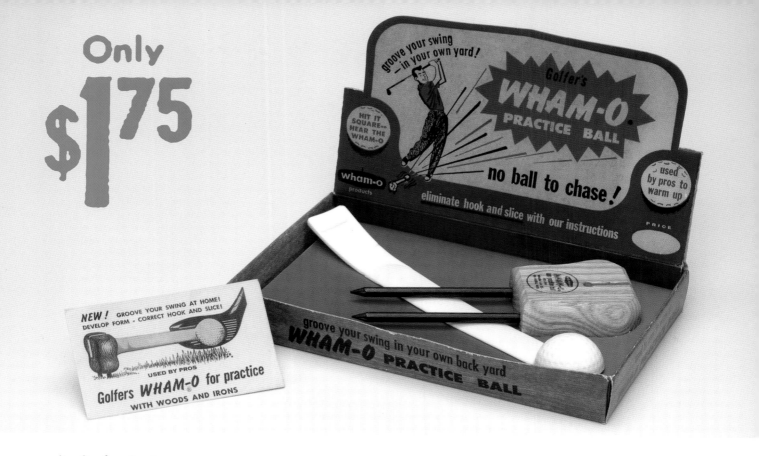

NEW! GROOVE YOUR SWING AT HOME!
DEVELOP FORM – CORRECT HOOK AND SLICE!

USED BY PROS

Golfers **WHAM-O** for practice
WITH WOODS AND IRONS

groove your swing — in your own yard!

Golfer's
WHAM-O
PRACTICE BALL

HIT IT SQUARE — HEAR THE WHAM-O

no ball to chase!

wham-o products

used by pros to warm up

PRICE

eliminate hook and slice with our instructions

groove your swing in your own back yard
WHAM-O PRACTICE BALL

WHAM-O TETHER BASEBALL TRAINER
no ball to chase!

#122
#122-A

APPROVED FOR LITTLE LEAGUE

teaches How to Hit!

It's fun to bat the ball again and again. Both father and son can enjoy this baseball practice game. One player twirls the ball through the strike zone and the other player slugs the ball. 20 hits out of 30 strikes wins the game. Sharpens the eye for hitting and bunting. The whole family can play right in the back yard.

STANDARD
$1.25
122A

DELUXE
$1.98
122

WHAM-O® tether game

Competitive Sport! Family Fun!

Skill game for all ages! Wonderful exercise — swell for parties. Set up anywhere in yard.

$3.98

Players bat ball in opposite directions. Winner hits ball past opponent until it winds up on the pole.

2 paddles, cord, ball, and 3-piece pole

WHAM-O New FLOOR TENNIS

PLAY INDOORS OR OUTDOORS

OR USE ANY TABLE—

It's really fun! Special light ball travels more slowly than ping-pong ball—long rallies are easy! It's portable — sets up in a minute. Plays like table tennis but there is no bulky table to get in the way. Play indoors or outdoors. Kids love the game. Set comes complete with paddles, net, brackets, court mark.

COMPLETE . . . . . $2.98 RETAIL

Exciting Game-Kids love it!

SET ON TABLE OR FLOOR

WHAM-O New SNOWBALL game

You can hardly miss— it almost floats!

THE BEST OF TENNIS— THE BEST OF BADMINTON!

$9.95

Long rallies are easy — everybody looks good! Like tennis, the ball can be played in the air or on the bounce. Use "cut shots" to make the ball curve. Court sets up in five minutes, comes complete with court lines, paddles, balls, poles, net, stakes and rules.

Fun for everybody. play on grass, cement, dirt

WHAM-IT

2 PADDLES AND BIRD

in two sizes..

$1.98

98¢

BADMINTON No court necessary

SKILL GAME .. KEEP SCORE

RALLY ANYWHERE .. IN THE BACKYARD .. AT THE BEACH .. ON CEMENT OR GRASS .. OR IN THE GAME ROOM .. GREAT FOR PARTIES, TOO!

PLAY OVER NET OR CORD BETWEEN POLES. SCORE LIKE BADMINTON, EASY TO CONTROL. EVERYBODY PLAYS .. YOUNG AND OLD

In the late '50s and early '60s, several products were introduced to help athletes improve their game, including Tether Baseball and the Golfer's Practice Ball, the latter promoting a way to "groove your swing in your own back yard." Both made practice fun with "no ball to chase." To help the stay-at-home athlete, there was the Swedish Method Figure Beauty Developer. More than a mouthful, it was a vintage attempt at a home fitness device, made with surgical rubber tubing and wooden handles.

WHAM-O's biggest contribution to backyard sports came in the form of paddle games. The company must have gotten a really good deal on wooden paddles, because no less than four early games feature them! There was the Tether Game, Floor Tennis (which "plays like table tennis but there is no bulky table to get in the way"), WHAM-IT (which featured an oversized bird that later became the New Giant Tennis Bird), and a game called Snowball. The Tether Game was "swell for parties," Floor Tennis made "long rallies easy," WHAM-IT was "easy to control," the Giant Tennis Bird guaranteed "more fun than ever," and the Snowball Game? The package promised: "You can hardly miss it—it almost floats."

ABOVE: WHAM-O's early offerings featured a plethora of paddle games.

OPPOSITE TOP: "HIT IT SQUARE— HEAR THE 'WHAM-O'!"

OPPOSITE BOTTOM: Many a dad must have taken one for the team when using WHAM-O's Tether Baseball from 1958. Sure, there's no ball to chase because it's attached to the rope wrapped around Dad's neck!

PAGE 36: A model shows off her Trac-Ball technique in this publicity photo from the late '70s.

IT'S **WHAM-O** BIG BIRD THAT MAKES EVERYONE AN EXPERT

Big Bird

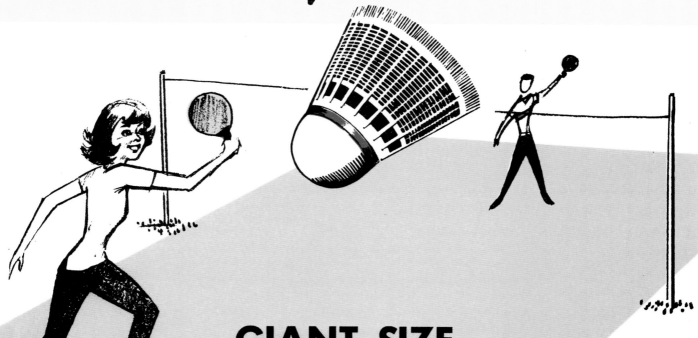

GIANT SIZE

SHUTTLE COCK . . . 5 inches

NEW FUN -- EXCITING ACTION!

PLAY LIKE BADMINTON, WITH
OR WITHOUT NET PLAY FOR
POINTS, HAVE LONG RALLIES
PLAY ANYWHERE.

WHAM-O "SMART BELLS"
the dumbbell you fill with water

ADJUSTABLE WEIGHT

2 FOR $1.98

KEEPS YOU FIT - Smart Bells do the trick! Gain weight, build muscles, lose excess fat, feel fit

SCIENTIFICALLY DESIGNED - for scientific development. Increase the weight as you progress

LESS EXPENSIVE - MORE EFFICIENT - the practical dumbell . . . fun for the whole family!

THEY'RE FUN AT THE BEACH - Just fill with sand
LIGHTWEIGHT FOR TRAVEL - and easy storage

figure beauty with "SMART BELLES"

2 FOR $1.98

Smart Figure!
Smart Girl!
She uses Smart Belles!

FUN TO USE! Smart belles help themselves to that dream silhouette. Makes exercise easy and fun. Simply fill Smart Belles to desired weight as you progress. Helps a girl regain a firmer, more graceful figure in the privacy of her home. Durable, attractive 10" long, adjustable weight. Pink color.

OPPOSITE: WHAM-O's oversized badminton bird was used in its WHAM-IT game before going solo as the New Giant Tennis Bird, then Big Bird. More significantly, it marked the beginning of WHAM-O's love of producing oversized fun. Soon came New Giant Tiddly Winks, Monster Magnet, Giant Monster Bubbles, and Super Balloon, among others.

LEFT: WHAM-O's water-filled bowling accessories were followed up with dumbbells you filled with water. Smart Bells were for men and Smart "Belles" for the ladies who wanted "that dream silhouette."

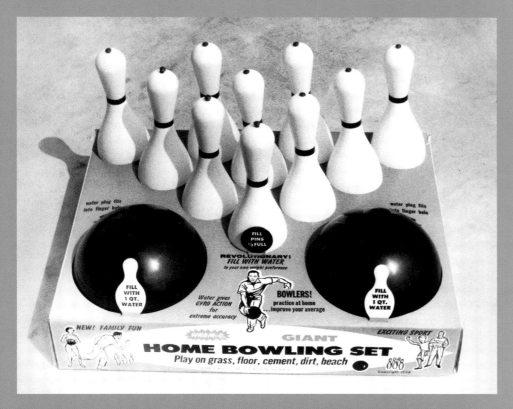

water plug fits into finger hole

FILL PINS 1/3 FULL

REVOLUTIONARY! **FILL WITH WATER** to your own weight preference

FILL WITH 1 QT. WATER

Water gives GYRO ACTION for extreme accuracy

BOWLERS! practice at home . . . improve your average

water plug fits into finger hole

FILL WITH 1 QT. WATER

NEW! FAMILY FUN · GIANT · EXCITING SPORT

HOME BOWLING SET
Play on grass, floor, cement, dirt, beach

play on grass, cement, dirt
use cans or milk cartons

REG. SIZE

BOWLERS! PRACTICE AT HOME DEVELOP SKILL

$2.50

As much fun as a bowling alley right in your backyard!

Trac-Ball®

A new dimension in a racquet game. An exciting sport for the backyard, beach or park.

Features 2 scientifically designed racquets that deliver super control, spins and curves. Plus 4 balls.

The special engineering of the racquets lets the players trap, catch and throw the ball in one continuous motion.

Totally self-contained, the game can be played anywhere there is some open space.

WHAM-O's ability to give people more affordable versions of popular sports was an early theme. Bowling was popular in the 1950s, but a home bowling set was impractical. So to give people some realism, Wham-O licensed an ingenious idea from Frisbee inventor Fred Morrison—a hollow, plastic bowling ball that could be filled with a quart of water to make it heavy. At first Rich and Spud encouraged people to make their own pins using cans or milk cartons. Later, WHAM-O provided ten hollow plastic pins with the game that could also be filled with water.

Around the same time, Shuffleboard became popular at Florida hotels and on cruise ships. But how do you play the game without the smooth concrete court? With Lawn Shuffle, a game featuring pucks capable of sliding on flat surfaces or rolling over lawns. For those who wanted a cheaper version they could play on their floor or patio, there was Scoot Shuffleboard.

These sporting products were all well and good, but to really distinguish itself as an innovator, WHAM-O had to create something new. The company did just that with an enduring WHAM-O product first released in 1975. Trac-Ball was touted as "an exciting innovation for individual, team, or family sport." How you play it individually, I don't know, but with a friend it sure was fun.

The curved basket of the racquet featured a ridged plastic "track" that gave the ball its spin and the sport its name. The balls were "air-action" balls, which would bank and curve when launched. The yellow ones, made of hollow plastic, curved acceptably, but the white ones, which were made of dense Styrofoam (in early sets), curved spectacularly with the right wrist action.

Of all the WHAM-O sports products, two stand out: The Frisbee disc and Hacky Sack footbag have stood the test of time and continue to have a vast following. Frisbee's contribution to the sporting world will be explored in depth in the "Frisbee" chapter. For now, let's focus on the world-famous footbag.

OPPOSITE: Trac-Ball featured a "racquet" that acted as both a basket to catch the ball and a curved scoop to throw it.

LEFT: By 1980, Trac-Ball was a genuine hit, advertised nationally on TV and well on its way to classic status. This page is from WHAM-O's 1980 catalog.

WHAM-O bought the rights to Hacky Sack footbags in 1983, but the origin of the sport began in the summer of 1972, when Mike Marshall showed fellow Oregonian John Stalberger a game where you kick a beanbag lightly in the air, trying to keep it off the ground as long as possible.

"I'd juggled soccer balls before [using just my feet], but when Mike started juggling his beanbag," Stalberger said, "I was like, 'Wow! That's cool.'" Stalberger was in the process of rehabilitating an injured knee when he was introduced to Marshall and his bag of tricks. After six months of playing footbag, Stalberger's knee had recuperated, and the proficiency with which he and Marshall could "hack the sack" soon garnered attention from anyone who saw the pair in action. It wasn't long before the two men decided to take the idea further. The result was Hacky Sack.

Marshall and Stalberger launched their business in 1974 with beanbags that were square and made by hand at first. "We would use all kinds of filler that was organic—beans, rice, whatever," Stalberger said. Over time, the filler changed to glass buttons, something the partners could buy in bulk at a cheap price. "The problem with the buttons was that they would break apart over time and they'd end up becoming sand," Stalberger recalled. "Ironically, nowadays the most popular filler *is* sand."

With their patent filed and sales beginning, things were looking promising for the two entrepreneurs when an inconceivable tragedy struck. Mike Marshall had a heart attack and died at the age of 28. His death had a lasting effect on his friend and business partner, and for a time it seemed as though the dream of spreading Hacky Sack would die with its originator.

"The first time I met Mike it was an instant friendship. I can't say that I've ever had that happen before or since," Stalberger shared. "His death was devastating." Asked how he carried on without his friend, Stalberger said, "I got encouragement from our mutual friends for sure, but I also believe that God told me to finish what Mike and I had started."

OPPOSITE LEFT: To differentiate its footbag from the many others flooding the market, WHAM-O marketed this Hacky Sack as a soccer training aid.

OPPOSITE CENTER: The Original Hacky Sack, circa 1975 (FB stands for footbag). It's ironic that the same company that made the high-bounce Super-Ball also helped popularize a product patented for its overt unbounciness. Leave it to WHAM-O to blow us away with a beanbag.

OPPOSITE RIGHT: In 1983, Stalberger sold his company to WHAM-O, and this version of the Hacky Sack footbag was produced shortly thereafter.

LEFT: Hacky Sack coinventor John Stalberger shows off his footbag form.

With divine inspiration and the encouragement of family and friends, Stalberger formed the National Hacky Sack Company after Marshall's death. He hit the schools in and around Portland, and soon kids began asking local sporting goods stores for the "footbag" they'd seen demonstrated in their gym classes. The media soon heard about the new game/sport that was being played across Portland. As more Hacky Sacks were sold, the buzz garnered the National Hacky Sack Company national attention. In 1979, Stalberger appeared on *Good Morning America*, and the game of footbag was well on its way.

Stalberger's company sold over 2 million Hacky Sack footbags from 1972 to 1983, and the sport became an underground hit not only in grade schools, but also on college campuses. The noncompetitive nature of Hacky Sack drew people into circles of strangers, who soon became friends. The term "Getting the Hack" meant that each person in the circle touched the sack before it hit the ground. Success depended on every player's contribution, and of course, good passing skills. Conversing during a Frisbee toss was more akin to shouting at one another, but the close proximity of the players in footbag made the friendly game an intimate social experience.

Now there's a World Footbag Association that publishes the magazine *Footbag World*, and the official governing body of the sport, the International Footbag Committee (IFC), sanctions the rules. It is estimated that over 25 million footbags have been sold since Mike Marshall and John Stalberger's first handmade sacks hit the scene in 1972.

Not many people can say that they helped invent a sport. John Stalberger is one of them. "The most important thing to me over the years has been the relationships that have developed because of Hacky Sack and the sport of footbag. Many lasting friendships and even marriages have come out of this thing. These couples have kids, and now their kids are kicking, too. That's a pretty awesome thing when you stop to think about it." When Stalberger stops to think about it, he often thinks of Mike Marshall. "His spirit is still here," he says. "Oh yeah, I see Mike all the time."

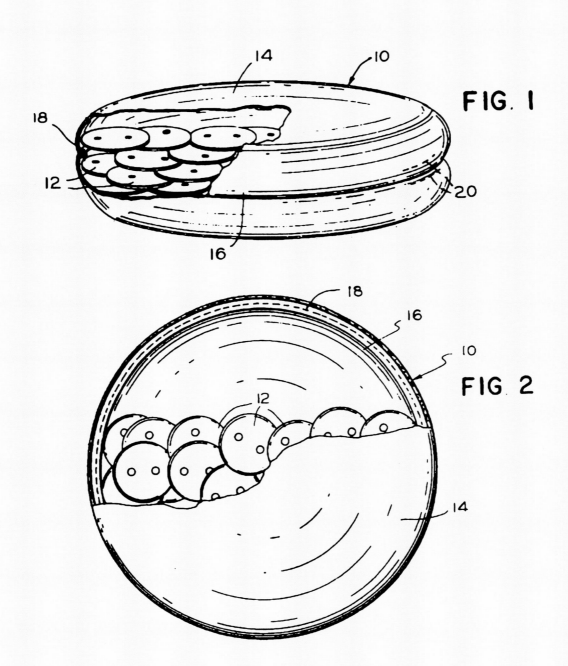

FIG. 1

FIG. 2

WHAM-O

- CONTEMPORARY DESIGN
- EASY-TO-CLEAN PLASTIC
- PINK, AQUA, YELLOW, WHITE

hi·n·dry
SOAP DISH

©

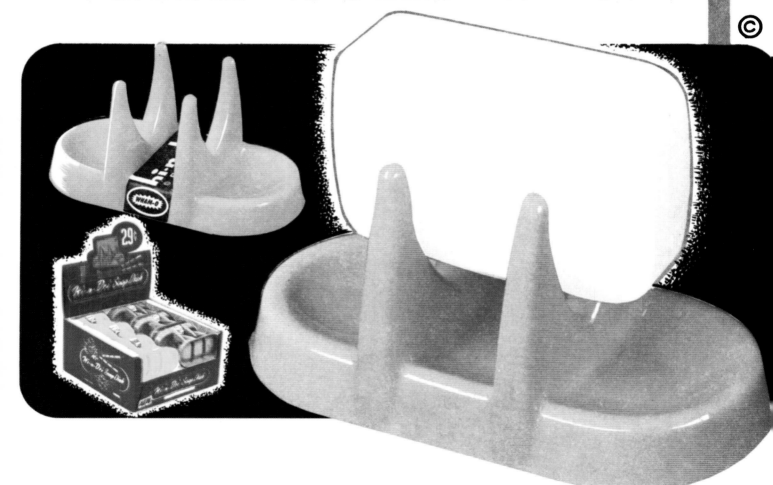

4

Why Not?

Only 98¢

This chapter was not originally planned. Since this book is primarily about WHAM-O toys, sporting goods, and novelties, why even cover non-toy products? Many toy companies have diversified their product lines in the past. Tonka made garden tools. The Flexible Flyer sled company made seed spreaders. Play-Doh began as a commercial wallpaper cleaner within the very clean walls of a soap company. But with WHAM-O, there was a twisted sense of fun in their non-toy products that warrants inclusion. Before SuperBall there was the SunVu, and before Hula Hoop there was Mr. Hootie.

PAGE 48: A mere 29 cents was all it took to keep your soap from getting slimey, thanks to WHAM-O's Hi-N-Dry Soap Dish.

BELOW: WHAM-O entered the kitchen-and-bar utensil field in 1957, riding on the coat-tails of the rather scary and bizarre Mr. Hootie.

The Fabulous Mr. Hootie Rake (Kitchen and Bar Tool) comes right out of a fever dream. It was a utensil (supposedly popular in Paris) designed to remove the white stringy things attached to egg yolks. In cooking circles, these small tissues are called "chalaza," from the Greek *khalaza*, or "small knot." Some cooks believe the larger the chalaza, the fresher the egg. Spud disagreed. He called them "woogers, hooties, string gloobers," and thought they were nasty. "Mr. Hootie was Spud's idea," Rich said. "He thought he could get everyone excited about the little thing that attached the yolk to the egg. 'Course, it was all in his head," he laughed, adding after a pause, "Hey, our sense of humor is what keeps us alive." The Mr. Hootie Rake was advertised with a mink belt holster for it, but don't dismiss that as just a joke. Spud and Rich also sold mink and suede leather through WHAM-O's mail-order division.

fabulous **MR. HOOTIE RAKE**
KITCHEN AND BAR TOOL

the ONLY wooger snatcher for eggs!
takes egg woogers and bits of egg shell off the yolk quickly and neatly

It's so continen

READ WHY THIS IS SO POPULAR IN PARIS

WOOG

ATTACKS ONIONS, OLIVES, BAR FRUIT
in small jars *WITHOUT FEAR*

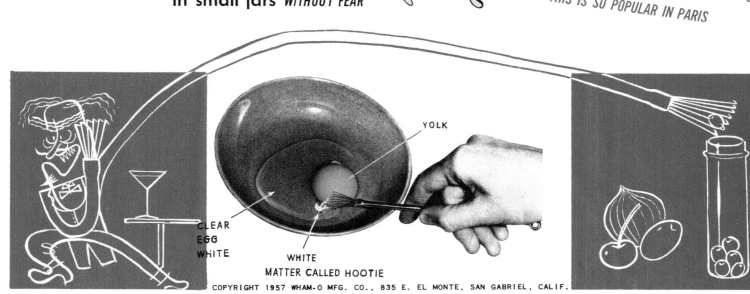

YOLK

CLEAR
EGG
WHITE

WHITE
MATTER CALLED HOOTIE

COPYRIGHT 1957 WHAM-O MFG. CO., 835 E. EL MONTE, SAN GABRIEL, CALIF.
PHONE: CUMBERLAND 3-1265

Rich and Spud brought a toy company's sense of fun to their non-toy products, with tongues planted firmly in cheeks. But there was also a strangeness to these products that made you wonder if they were really serious about selling them. Did they really think the Mr. Hootie Rake would be big? But while some ask "Why?" the WHAM-O founders often said, "Why not?" Many of WHAM-O's non-toy items had grown-up uses. The Mr. Hootie Rake was also a bar tool that "attacks onions, olives, bar fruit in small jars without fear." It was a tool that fit right in with the company's Chain Gang Coasters.

The Chain Gang coasters were a collection of hollow, plastic drink coasters with cartoon characters whose expressions altered when their wiggly, chain-link mouths changed shape. "The picture changes when you jiggle the coaster!" the packaging declared, all the while promoting martini drinking and swimsuit-model ogling.

BELOW: Chain Gang drinking coasters from 1958. Smile or Frown? It depended on the chain's reaction.

You might be drinking, too, if you thought that nuclear annihilation was imminent. One legend, found on Web sites and in news stories, is that WHAM-O made a "Do-it-yourself bomb shelter." WHAM-O's own Web site says, "During the great bomb shelter craze of the 1960s, the company marketed the plans and parts for a $119 do-it-yourself shelter." Not having lived through the "duck and cover" era, I found such a product hard to believe. Then I discovered the ad for it.

It cost "$179 delivered," and was technically a "Bomb Fallout Shelter Cover," not a shelter. The clue that Rich and Spud were behind this product was the fact that "Consolidated Research & Development Corp." had the same street address as WHAM-O. Rich confirmed it was indeed WHAM-O's doing. "Sure, we offered a bomb shelter for sale. It was during the war scare." Did they sell many? "Oh, no," he said with a laugh. "All you really did was buy the bricks from us and build your own."

Exotic Waterfall

EXOTIC PRODUCTS for HOME & GARDEN

WF 109

Giant South Sea Clam Shell Waterfall

Beautifully sculptured 3 tier Clam Shell Fountain, 20", 24" and 28" shells, replica of the giant clams found in the South Seas. A real showpiece that is portable for indoor or outdoor use. $49.95

Suggested Retail

$49.95

P-122
Clam Planter and Stand
Giant clam mounted on legs. Used as planter, as fishpond, or display.

TROPICAL ACCENTS

Interior wall and garden decorations made of hollow rugged styron. Exciting conversation pieces to lend charm and interest to your home and garden. Withstands weather and can be back-lighted for dramatic indirect wall lighting.

STAKE TABLE

ACCESSORY TABLE FOR BAR-B-Q

PORTABLE TABLE — JUST PUSH IN GROUND ANYWHERE

BACKYARD • CAMPERS

LAWN PARTIES • MAKES ENTERTAINING EASY — JUST RIGHT FOR HORS D'OEUVRES AND BEVERAGES.

use as a tray

• MOUNTAIN • BEACH

EASILY SET UP IN SECONDS . . . FOR CAMPING, MEALS • IDEAL FOR SMALL ITEMS — GLASSES, WATCHES, ETC. . . . KEEPS THEM OUT OF SAND.

washes like a plate

WHAM-O MFG. CO., SAN GABRIEL, CALIF.

WHAM-O was also worldly. "When the business started to make a little money, we traveled to lots of places," Rich recalled. "We went to the Caribbean, Africa—everywhere." These travels are reflected in WHAM-O's "Exotic" line of home decor items. "We were always looking for something unique . . . something that would sell," Spud explained. "We did a whole line of different waterfalls because they sold well."

Spud and Rich could never be accused of sitting on the sidelines of life. When they weren't thinking up their next product or traveling to look for it, they were hunting, fishing, boating, or camping. "We did a lot of that stuff," Rich remembered. Hence, WHAM-O sold several "outdoorsman" items such as the Fun Boat (a lightweight, portable boat that fit in the back of your pickup), the Stake Table (the accessory table for "BAR-B-Q"), the Hotspot Heater, and the Totalite Fluorescent Light (a portable light the company acquired when it purchased the Mentis Corporation in the mid-1960s). For eating outdoors, WHAM-O created the Picnic "Snap-Out" Set, featuring a plate, cup, and utensils, all molded in one piece for easy packing. They snapped apart when you were ready for a fireside or dockside meal.

In 1962, WHAM-O had a bumper crop of non-toy items. For the kitchen freezer there was the Frozen Sucker Mold (a "machine" for making homemade popsicles, created by Frisbee inventor Fred Morrison), and for the bathroom, the Hi-N-Dry Soap

OPPOSITE: You could accessorize anywhere with the Stake Table.

BELOW: WHAM-O's Frozen Sucker Mold from 1962 came with this advice: "If it tastes good and it's wet . . . FREEZE IT!"

FROZEN SUCKER MOLD

MMM!

Kids love em so-o-o-

Make your own

FROZEN SUCKERS

right at home

with this unique frozen sucker machine

Choose your favorite DELICIOUS FLAVORS

molds 8 large suckers
CUP-ON-STIK ENDS MESS

The original frozen sucker machine with perfected design

if it tastes good and it's wet . . . FREEZE IT!

98c

HAVE FUN . . .
SAVE MONEY!!

WHAM-O SUNVU

protects your face from Sun
at any angle!
NO OBSTRUCTED VIEW

COOL and LIGHTWEIGHT

OUTDOOR SPORTS

AT THE BEACH

AT THE GAME

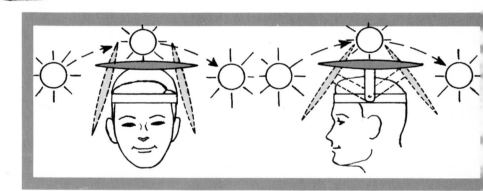

Carry it anywhere, FLAT. One twist — snaps into shape

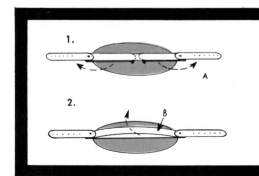

1. TURN END PIECES OUT AS IN "A."
2. LIFT "B", TWIST ON THE TWO ENDS.
3. SNAPS TO CORRECT HEAD SIZE.

© 1962

WHAM-O MFG. CO.   **835 E. EL MONTE ST., SAN GABRIEL, CALIF.**

Dish. "That was one of the first things that we marketed that we didn't know why in the hell we did it," Rich laughed, adding, "It was a neat item. We got it patented and it worked. It kept your soap dry on your sink."

The Pediatric Baby Seat and the Baby Bath Changer came next. "We started to sell an awful lot of stuff for little kids," Rich said. The new direction led to a keepsake product called Precious Prints. It featured a clay-like compound that you used to take an impression of your child's hand or foot. You then baked it in the oven at 350° for 10 minutes to make a permanent 3-D print that you could display in the enclosed frame.

WHAM-O produced many ads and flyers over the years that were suitable for framing, but one stands above the rest. Style had a new name in 1962, and it was SunVu. Literally a translucent, plastic green disc that you strapped to your head, the swiveling SunVu was part visor, part sunglasses, and totally WHAM-O.

Too self-conscious to wear a SunVu? Then perhaps WHAM-O could convince you to wear a bonnet made of bows. "Bowmatic—now, that was a good product!" Rich enthused. "It was out of line with what we usually did, but a woman could make all kinds of things." The Bowmatic was marketed directly to women, promising "the art of bowmaking made easy" and bows that "blossom at your magic touch." Of course,

OPPOSITE: The SunVu was cool at any angle. The expression on the face of the poor fella "at the game" baking in the sun is especially entertaining. Dude, you can carry your SunVu anywhere, *flat*. What were you thinking?

BELOW: Straight from the land of Ron Popeil's Veg-O-Matic and Dial-O-Matic came WHAM-O's Bowmatic in 1963.

NEW INSTANT
STRING-A-TREE
U.S. PAT. PEND
TM

Sprays beautiful flowing decorative ribbon string!

NON-FLAMMABLE
FLUORESCENT
COLORS
GLOWS UNDER
BLACK LIGHT

WR

CENTER

STOCK No. 415   **NET WEIGHT 4 OZ.**

CAUTION: CONTENTS UNDER PRESSURE. SEE CAUTION ON BACK.

just making bows wasn't enough to justify this expensive machine, so WHAM-O didn't refer to them as merely bows; they were "colorful creations with hundreds of uses . . . as stunning accents for hair, dresses, or even glamorous hats."

When asked if his heart was in these non-toys, or whether he enjoyed making toys better, Rich's answer is surprising: "I wouldn't say we liked toys better. All we wanted to do was find something that would sell. It was exciting. We were entrepreneurs." After a long pause, he added, "Spud and I had fun. We had a lot of fun doing what we did. We loved it. Whether it paid off or not, it didn't matter. We had fun."

5

Amazing action—

hula·hoop

**Rotates perpetually
with body-english**

In 1958, WHAM-O was an established sporting goods manufacturer with an emphasis on novelty weapons. Not your typical profile for a company that was about to launch the biggest toy craze the world had ever seen. The stage was already set in Australia, where a company called Toltoys had produced the first plastic hoop (and sold a reported four hundred thousand of them) in 1957. Toltoys' president, Alex Tolmer, brought the idea to Rich and Spud, and in the spring of 1958, WHAM-O made Whoopee.

PAGE 60: In 1958, Spud and Rich apparently produced (or at least contemplated producing) the Whoopee Hoop under the company name S&R Research before calling it Hula Hoop. Pictured here is the cardboard label that would have been stapled around the hoop.

OPPOSITE TOP: To supplement its regular production, WHAM-O hired high school and college students to make hoops during their summer break, but still couldn't keep up with orders.

OPPOSITE BOTTOM: At the height of the craze, it was as if the Hula Hoop had the world under a witch doctor's spell. WHAMBO was an "African Pigmy Witch Doctor" in a culturally insensitive time. He was used in ads and on packaging for several WHAM-O toys.

It's hard to imagine that the WHAM-O Hula Hoop was almost the S&R Research Whoopee Hoop. Apparently Rich and Spud had decided to start their toy division under a different name than WHAM-O. This was also around the time that they changed their sporting goods division name to "WAMO." "S&R stood for Spud & Rich," Rich revealed. "After all that nonsense with different names, it was always one thing: WHAM-O and nothing else."

Hoops as toys have been around for thousands of years, fashioned out of things like dried vines and bamboo. The origin of the name "Hula Hoop" is a little easier to pinpoint, but not much. Some historians credit British sailors, who visited the Hawaiian Islands in the 1800s, as coining the phrase, but according to *Panati's Extraordinary Origins of Everyday Things*, by Charles Panati, the term "hula" was first associated with the game of keeping a hoop twirling around one's waist in the 1700s. He says, "Then, hula was a sensuous, mimetic Hawaiian dance, performed sitting or standing, with undulating hip gestures . . . the dance's hip gyrations so perfectly matched the motions required to rotate a toy hoop that 'hula' became the name of the game." I asked Rich where the famous name came from, and he said, "I'll tell you where it came from—right out of our minds! I remember the circumstances. Spud and I were discussing what to call it, 'Hula Hoop' or some other name, and my dad was walking out of the office and overheard us and said, 'Oh, make up your minds!' So I said, 'Okay, Hula Hoop. That's it.' And that was that."

Spud and his wife, Suzy, demonstrated the newly named Hula Hoop to "trendsetting kids" in local parks and schools around San Gabriel, to ever-increasing sales. "We put the Hula Hoop in a local shop on consignment and then went to my daughter's grammar school," Suzy Melin said. "We taught the kids on the playground how to do the Hula Hoop and where to go buy them. That's how we started it." From there the couple worked to get their toy on TV. "Spud and I went on TV shows together," Melin recalled. "We'd just cold call them. We'd show up and demonstrate the Hula Hoops and ask to be on the show. It was 1958 and studios were wide open to that sort of thing. We got on a lot of shows."

When Dinah Shore featured the gravity-defying hoops on her national TV show, she unknowingly sparked a phenomenon. An article from *Life*, which ran on September 8, 1958, reported that, "Hoops, powered by hips and a refreshing lack of inhibition, were spinning everywhere last week. The brightly colored plastic rings, three feet in diameter and variously called 'Hula Hoops,' 'Spin-A-Hoops,' and 'Hoop-de-dos,' were orbiting around four million undulating torsos in backyards, on playgrounds and beaches, at barbecues and cocktail parties all over the U.S." The article credited Spud and the "Wham-O Manufacturing Company" for beginning the craze before noting, "40 or more novelty makers hopped on the hoop wagon, and sales . . . are expected to total 15 million by November." The *Life* article was only off by about 65 million hoops.

The generic hoop was thought to be unpatentable, so it's no wonder so many different hoop toys were released in 1958. Scores of toy companies smelled profit in

NUINE WHAM-O ORIGINAL

hula-hoop

WHAMBO SAYS:
Cool witch doctors do the Lil' Hula
Hoopee and the Wham-O Whing
Ding along with the Hula Hoop.

AMAZING...DEFIES GRAVITY

ending WHAM-O MFG. CO., SAN GABRIEL, CALIF.

1958 WHAM-O Mfg. Co., 835 E. El Monte St. San Gabriel, California • Cumberland 3-1265

GENUINE WHAM-O ORIGINAL

hula-hoop

WHAMBO SAYS:
Cool witch doctors do the Lil' Hula
Hoopee and the Wham-O Whing
Ding along with the Hula Hoop.

AMAZING...DEFIES GRAVITY

Patent Pending WHAM-O MFG. CO., SAN GABRIEL, CALIF.

Copyright 1958 WHAM-O Mfg. Co., 835 E. El Monte St. San Gabriel, California • Cumberland 3-1265

all that spinning plastic. With estimates ranging from 80 to 100 million hoops sold, it was a fad of epic proportions. Hooper Doopers were sold. Wiggle-A-Hoops were sold. Marx Toys, the biggest toy company in the world in 1958, sold Hoop Zings. Even TV personality Art Linkletter "hopped on the hoop wagon." He is credited as the inventor of the Hula Hoop in articles on the Internet and has claimed in interviews to have "backed it." In a 2002 article from *Time* magazine it was reported, "Linkletter also introduced the Hula Hoop in the U.S." But Linkletter introduced the above mentioned Spin-A-Hoop, not the Hula Hoop. When asked for clarification on Linkletter's involvement, Rich's response was predictable. "He was a big phony. I hate to use those words about a guy, but that's what he was. He said that he originated it, and he had nothing to do with it. He was just one of the many people who knocked it off."

According to the U.S. Patent and Trademark Office, WHAM-O first used the trademark "Hula Hoop" on May 21, 1958. They've owned it ever since, and saying that all the other hoops that sold in 1958 were Hula Hoops is like saying all rag dolls are Raggedy Ann or all modeling compounds are Play-Doh. Knock-offs are prevalent in the toy industry (see chapter ten, "Super Toys,"), but trademarks rule. By all accounts, the most hoops sold by a single company in the craze of 1958 were by WHAM-O. Although it's estimated that the company sold 25 million Hula Hoops that year, it was only about 25 to 35 percent of the total number sold. WHAM-O could have accounted for more, but it just couldn't keep up with demand.

"We never realized that Hula Hoop was ever going to be as big as it was," Rich said. "Most of them were made in our plant, but we subcontracted it everywhere. We hired machine time to have them made in Cleveland, Chicago—everywhere. We had seven plants running all 'round the world."

The international world discovered Hula Hoop, too. In December 1958, *Time* reported, "The bright plastic things were to be seen everywhere—along Paris' Champs-Elysees, in the stodgiest of London shops, in the geisha houses of Tokyo, even among the smart luggage of the Queen Mother Zaine of Jordan, who was on her way home. Prime Minister Kishi of Japan got one for his 62nd birthday. . . . Not since the yo-yo had a U.S. craze spread so far so fast. The Hula Hoop had circled the globe." It was also sold in Poland, Finland, and Germany. Back in America, Hula Hoop marathons were staged; songs about it were being released. The entire planet, it seemed, was loopy for the Hula Hoop.

One reason so many Hula Hoops were sold was the appeal of spinning as many hoops as possible. You can imagine a kid saying, "Hey Dad, Billy spun ten Hula Hoops at once. Can I have money to buy five more?" Rich shared that the key to WHAM-O's success was coming up with other things you could do beyond just spinning the Hula Hoop around your waist. "We figured out a lot of tricks you could do with it," he said. That was confirmed by an early Hula Hoop TV ad: "Just give it a spin and do lots of tricks. Around the neck is called 'Kill the Buzzard.' Around your waist, 'The Natural.' Slip it way down and do 'The Knee-knocker.' It's easy to do 'The Stork.' Play 'War'. . . . It's fun to skip with your WHAM-O Hula Hoop. . . . Quick now, run through your Hula

OPPOSITE: In another marketing bonanza for WHAM-O, the company took a page from Duncan Yo-Yos and ran contests across the country. Here we have "The Knee-knocker," "The Natural," and "Kill the Buzzard," performed by some expert Hula Hoopsters, circa 1958.

BELOW: The fun of Hula Hoop was super-sized in late 1958 with the new Giant Hula Hoop. Note that these kids also sport Hula Hats.

Hoop, even play giant horseshoes. . . . Do the amazing 'Upsy-Daisy'. . . . Get one, get two, get more! It's the new amazing WHAM-O Hula Hoop."

Since everyone and their brother seemed to be making "hoops," and since that word was too generic to trademark, the word "hula" was paramount. WHAM-O scrambled to expand its product line: in the company's catalog dated November 1, 1958, there was the Lil' Hula-Hoopee ("the little brother to the famous WHAM-O Hula Hoop"), Hula Board ("more fun than riding a bucking bronco"), and even the silly Hula Hat ("the world's coolest four-shaped mad hat!").

it's convertible -four shapes

PARTY FUN!

IT'S CRAZY – IT'S COOL!

HULA HAT
by the makers of famous HULA-HOOP

no sizes . . this one fits your head !

the world's coolest four-shaped mad hat! Captured from Whambo, the African Pigmy Witch Doctor who does the Hula-Hoop . . . Get several, Mom will want one, Dad will snitch one for fishing and Sis will take it to the beach. It's the world's coolest (and nattiest) hat!. . THE HULA HAT

WHAM-O
push O hoop
made by the makers of famous Hula Hoop

Barrels of fun with no practice at all !

COUNTLESS GAMES:
RACES, HORSESHOES,
ROLL-AND-CATCH
OBSTACLE COURSE

You, too, can be a famous Push-O-Hoop racer! Be the first in your neighborhood with this latest fad. Great transportation—run errands twice as fast! Wholesome exercise —improves coordination.

ROLL AND CATCH

OBSTACLE COURSE

RACES

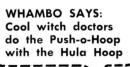

HORSESHOES

WHAMBO SAYS:
Cool witch doctors
do the Push-o-Hoop
with the Hula Hoop

Copyright Wham-O Mfg. Co.
E. El Monte St., San Gabriel, Calif.   PRINTED IN U.S.A.   **Wham-O Mfg. Co., San Gabriel, Calif.**

RIGHT: In college, you've got to learn to multitask. Here a student's body is divided as he sports a Hula Hat while twirling a Whing-Ding, swirling a Hula Hoop, and rocking a Hula Board.

SATELLITE SPINNER

DOUBLE WHING DING HULA

OVER THE TOP

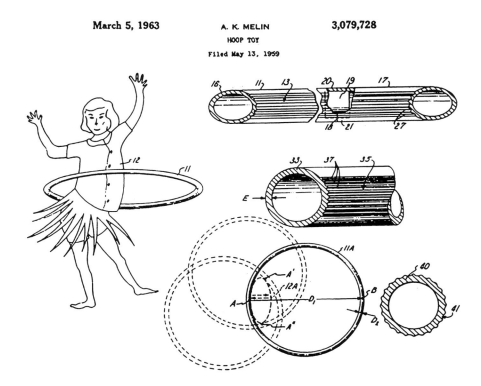

March 5, 1963   A. K. MELIN   3,079,728

HOOP TOY

Filed May 13, 1959

LEFT: Spud had just filed for his patent on the Hula Hoop when the fad fizzled.

Next came the Giant Hula Hoop. Four feet in diameter, it was "Extra Large for Adults," and easier to spin. Too big to sell at retail in one piece, WHAM-O sold it in sections and dubbed it "adjustable." Given the number of adult injuries reported at the height of the craze, from hernias to herniated disks, it's a good thing this hoop was limited to "kids 6 to 60."

At the height of the craze, WHAM-O was making twenty thousand Hula Hoops a week, in addition to all the production it farmed out. Then, without warning, the floodgates slammed shut. *The Wall Street Journal* reported, "Hoops Have Had It." In the book *A Toy Is Born*, author Marvin Kaye writes, "With tons of raw material on order and massive quantities of hoops being shipped out, the company found the orders simply stopped. There was no warning; one day everybody wanted Hula Hoops, the next day, demand was zero." In less than a year, Hula Hoop had sold faster and then died quicker than any other toy in history, becoming one of the biggest fads ever.

"We got stuck with a lot of them," Rich related. "We damn near went broke. It was born in January and dead as a doornail by October. We eventually got out of all the excess inventory, but it took a long time." This is the most amazing part of the Hula Hoop story—the fact that WHAM-O survived it. "It was probably the biggest toy that ever happened in the world," Rich said. "Probably the biggest that ever will."

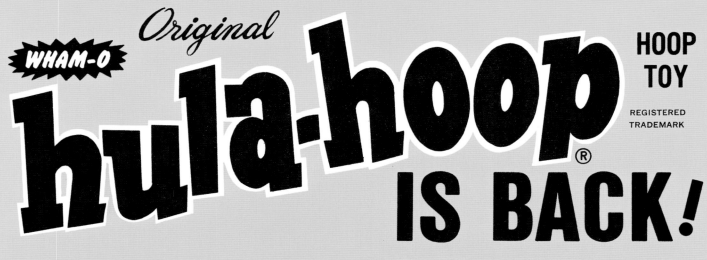

Original **WHAM-O** **hula-hoop®** HOOP TOY

REGISTERED TRADEMARK

IS BACK!

READY FOR THE *NEW* GENERATION!

U.S. PATENT PROTECTED

MECHANICAL PATENT
No. 3079728

Spud had applied for a patent covering the Hula Hoop's weight, diameter, and shape just as the Hula Hoop craze ended. When the patent was finally granted, most of the knock-off companies were already out of the hoop business, but that didn't stop Rich and Spud. They waited for five years, and then brought the Hula Hoop back.

In 1963, the Hula Hoop made a comeback, with a patent in place to protect it. Rich and Spud's new label warned, "IF IT'S NOT WHAM-O, IT'S NOT A HULA HOOP!" Two years later the Shoop-Shoop Hula Hoop was introduced, and it's been in WHAM-O's line ever since. A common misconception is that Hula Hoops sold like crazy, died out, and are now on the level of Pet Rocks or Mood Rings—just another lame fad from a bygone era. History has shown that this is simply not true. "When we sold the company in '82, we were selling a million and a half Hula Hoops a year," Rich bragged. With the spotlight focused on other toys, the sensation had become a staple.

One of the ways WHAM-O survived the biggest fad in history was through marketing savvy and patience. Not to be overlooked was Rich and Spud's keen eye for product, for just as the Hula Hoop went rattling to the ground in 1958, another product within WHAM-O's line was just about to soar.

OPPOSITE: Once WHAM-O's patent was granted, the company pushed to re-establish the Hula Hoop "for a new generation."

BELOW: WHAM-O gave the Hula Hoop sound in 1965 by trapping several beads inside its hollow tubing. The resulting *shoop, shoop* sound inspired the name Shoop-Shoop Hula Hoop.

FLIES LIKE CRAZY!

FRISBEE

6

List all the proprietary playthings that have sold for over fifty consecutive years and you'll get a Who's Who of classic toys. Whittle that list down to toys that have sold over 200 million copies and only a few elite playthings like Barbie, Monopoly, and Frisbee remain. These are toys that deserve time-capsule status. Toys that, if shot into space and discovered by some alien race, would help define our uniquely human experience. *Human* experience? Ask yourself which of those playthings is enjoyed by a *different species* on the planet Earth, and only Frisbee remains—loved by dogs, humans, and maybe even some creatures in a flying saucer somewhere.

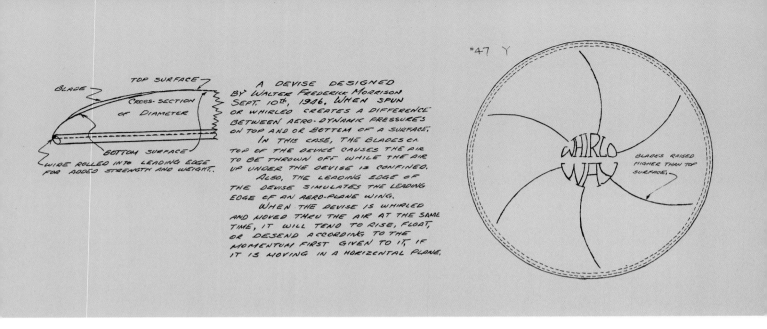

BLADE
TOP SURFACE
CROSS-SECTION OF DIAMETER
BOTTOM SURFACE
WIRE ROLLED INTO LEADING EDGE FOR ADDED STRENGTH AND WEIGHT.

A DEVISE DESIGNED BY WALTER FREDERICK MORRISON SEPT, 10TH, 1946. WHEN SPUN OR WHIRLED CREATES A DIFFERENCE BETWEEN AERO-DYNAMIC PRESSURES ON TOP AND OR BOTTOM OF A SURFACE;
IN THIS CASE, THE BLADES ON TOP OF THE DEVISE CAUSES THE AIR TO BE THROWN OFF WHILE THE AIR UP UNDER THE DEVISE IS CONFINED.
ALSO, THE LEADING EDGE OF THE DEVISE SIMULATES THE LEADING EDGE OF AN AERO-PLANE WING.
WHEN THE DEVISE IS WHIRLED AND MOVED THRU THE AIR AT THE SAME TIME, IT WILL TEND TO RISE, FLOAT, OR DESEND ACCORDING TO THE MOMENTUM FIRST GIVEN TO IT, IF IT IS MOVING IN A HORIZONTAL PLANE.

#47 Y

WHIRLO WAY

BLADES RAISED HIGHER THAN TOP SURFACE;

ABOVE: In 1946, Fred Morrison sketched out his idea for what would soon become the first plastic flying disc.

PAGE 72: Pie plates or "tins" from the Frisbee Pie Company were fun to throw and catch, making college kids in the late 1950s the first lovers of heavy metal.

Frisbee can trace its roots to a Thanksgiving Day picnic in 1937 when a high school student named Fred Morrison first tossed a metal popcorn can lid for fun. The path from Fred to Frisbee is a convoluted story across twenty years' worth of plastic platters and pie pans, Flyin-Saucers and family—much too time-consuming and twisted a tale for this book. Yet like Hacky Sack, the Frisbee had a life before it came into the WHAM-O fold, and it took on a life of its own after. So we'll attempt to share the saga succinctly, even if, like a Frisbee ricocheting off a sidewalk, we only skip along the surface of the story.

By 1938, Fred Morrison and his girlfriend Lucile Nay had graduated from high school as well as from tossing popcorn lids. They had moved on to cake pans. In his book written with Phil Kennedy, *Flat Flip Flies Straight!,* detailing the early story of Frisbee, Morrison writes, "The commercialization of airborne cake pans began one weekend on a Santa Monica, California, beach. We [Fred and Lu] were workin' up a sweat flyin' a pan, when an athletic-type sunbather . . . approached and offered to buy our plaything. We parted with the pan for twenty-five cents. . . . At the time cake pans cost about a nickel. Trading nickels for quarters had possibilities. A business was born!"

Fred and Lu's "Flyin' Cake Pan" enterprise was disrupted by World War II. Serving as an Army Air Corps pilot, Morrison survived being shot down and held as a POW outside Nuremberg, Germany. When he returned home in 1946, released from active duty, he was married to Lu, but jobless. Thinking back to his carefree days of "pan handling" on California beaches, Morrison sketched out an idea, proposing to marry the postwar emergence of plastic with the carefree cake pans of his youth. His "devise" [sic] had a "leading edge" like that of "an aero-plane wing." Alongside the

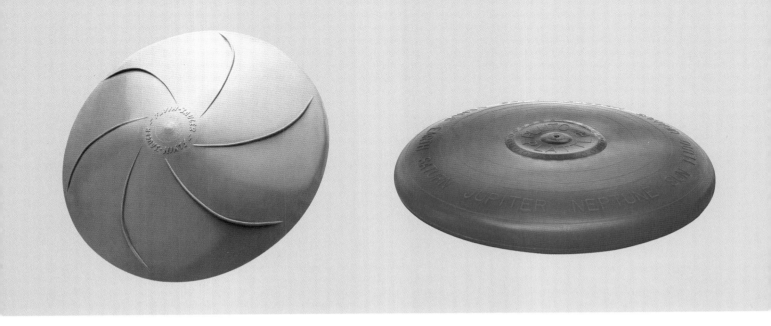

sketch, Morrison wrote, "When the devise [sic] is whirled and moved thru the air at the same time, it will tend to rise, float, or descend. . . ." For this reason he called it the Whirlo-Way.

With no money to make his idea a reality, Morrison took a job with a gas company owned by another former Air Force pilot named Warren Franscioni. The two men hit it off, and Morrison shared his idea with Franscioni. Seeing its potential, Franscioni agreed to fund the project, and a mold was made by a local plastics company to produce the toy. The year was 1947, and with the phenomenon of UFOs and the Roswell incident all making national headlines, the Whirlo-Way was renamed the "Flyin-Saucer."

It wasn't until 1948 that the mold based on Morrison's drawing was completed and the first Flyin-Saucers were released. That same year, WHAM-O was born in South Pasadena, less than five miles from Morrison and Franscioni's Glendale office. While Rich and Spud were out sawing slingshots, Fred and Warren were flinging Flyin-Saucers. The two men found that their new flying disc did not fly off store shelves unless it was demonstrated. The store manager of the local Woolworth's store in Glendale allowed the "World Champion Flyin-Saucer Pilots," as Morrison and Franscioni had dubbed themselves, to fly their saucers in his store, but only after they agreed to erect a barricade of chicken wire to protect his customers. In *Flat Flip Flies Straight!* Morrison tells the tale of what happened when a Flyin-Saucer crash-landed in Woolworth's. "A mis-tossed curving Saucer (mine) dove into and wiped out a fingernail polish display. The formerly delighted store manager came unglued. . . . His near-incoherent terminating remarks: 'Take those [expletive deleted] plastic things and get the [expletive deleted] out of my store! And, take that [expletive deleted] chicken-wire monstrosity with ya . . . NOW!'"

ABOVE LEFT: The predecessor to Frisbee, Morrison and Franscioni's Flyin-Saucer first soared in 1948.

ABOVE RIGHT: Fred Morrison's Pluto Platter looked more like a flying saucer than the Flyin-Saucer he and Franscioni had made.

The saucer pilots found fairer pastures for their venture in the great outdoors of county fairs. From the end of 1948 through 1949 they hit fairs across California, Arizona, and Florida. When someone wondered aloud if the discs were attached to wires to make them fly, Morrison and Franscioni incorporated the alleged ruse into their pitch: "100 feet of invisible wire sells for a penny a foot," they said, adding, "but the Flyin-Saucers are free." While sales were brisk at times, if a fair coincided with a windy day, their unstable, top-heavy disc did not fly well. After two years of disappointing sales, the partners parted ways in early 1950.

For four years, Morrison took odd jobs to make ends meet, including cooking meals on a shark boat and working in construction and carpentry. In 1954, he even purchased some Flyin-Saucers from the plastic company he and Franscioni had contracted with and sold them at the L.A. County Fair. He had such success there, this time with Lu and some friends helping him pitch the discs, that the idea of lowering his cost by making his own mold for a new disc seemed wise. In 1955, Morrison contracted with another plastics company and designed a mold for a new flying disc.

Morrison's new flying saucer looked like a UFO, complete with a raised cockpit in the center with tiny portholes. To further exploit the space-age theme, he had the mold maker engrave the name of the nine planets and the sun around the perimeter of his new platter. With Pluto having been recently discovered, Morrison settled on the name "Pluto Platter." Lu came up with the "instructions" for the new toy, molded right into the underside of every disc. The idea of needing instructions for something as ubiquitous as the Frisbee seems odd today, but in 1955 it had to be explained this way, "Play Catch—Invent Games. To fly, flip away backhanded. Flat flip flies straight. Tilted flip curves—experiment." The Pluto Platter was light-years ahead of the Flyin-Saucer in fashion (it looked cooler) and function (it flew better). The modern plastic flying disc was born.

"We saw [Fred] throwing it at the Los Angeles County Fair," Rich recalls. "He and his wife were having a catch, and that seemed to be attracting a crowd." At the time, Rich and Spud even contemplated molding their own disc. Then in 1956, someone who knew WHAM-O (no one can remember who) saw Morrison throwing Pluto Platters in a parking lot in L.A. and encouraged him to take his toy to the company. Morrison arranged for a meeting to show his unpatented disc to Rich and Spud. "We knew and they knew that they could go ahead and make their own plastic disc," Morrison related. "That left us in a very weak negotiating position." Rich recalled it this way: "We asked him [Fred] if we could take it over and pay him a royalty. After a little discussion, we had a deal."

From the time the plastic disc came into the WHAM-O fold, Rich and Spud recognized the importance of giving consumers games they could play with it beyond the game of catch. Their Pluto Platter Flying Saucer Horseshoe Game was one such idea. It came with four Pluto Platters, two wooden stakes, and a measuring cord. Later versions would include two additional "steel hoop targets," giving the horseshoe term "ringer" a whole new meaning. Also significant was the fact that the Pluto Platter

ABOVE: WHAM-O's Pluto Platter Flying Saucer Horseshoe Game is promoted in this publicity photo from 1957.

OPPOSITE: In 1955, Fred Morrison sold his Pluto Platter in a colorful bag with equally colorful copy. Note the not-so-safe suggestion to "Use bag for space helmet if head fits."

Flying Saucer Horseshoe Game introduced the idea of throwing plastic discs at a target, a play pattern that would have huge ramifications for the future of the plastic flying disc.

When WHAM-O first launched the Pluto Platter Flying Saucer, there was no mention of the word "Frisbee" anywhere on it, yet it was clear that Rich and Spud didn't like the name "Pluto Platter" from the start. While Morrison's packaging emphasized the name, WHAM-O's packaging emphasized many other words. Looking at early ads for the new toy it's clear that Rich and Spud didn't know what to call it.

To further confuse things, WHAM-O produced an entirely new, larger disc they called the "Sailing Satellite" in late 1957. Then, if all these name games weren't enough, along came Hula Hoop in 1958. The latter was such an incredible hit that production of plastic flying discs was severely reduced, if not halted within WHAM-O's plant. But Rich and Spud didn't ignore their new flying toy. In July 1958, they filed a trademark on the name "Frisbee."

The name "Frisbee" didn't appear out of nowhere. From 1949 to 1959, the Flyin-Saucer had many competitors in the space race of plastic flying discs. And no matter what these companies and entrepreneurs named their plastic discs—Space Saucer, Sky Pie, Super Saucer, Zo-Lar—people "out east" often called them "Frisbies." Why? Because of a pie company.

The Frisbie Pie Company was founded in 1871 in Bridgeport, Connecticut. It was a mainstay in New England until 1958, when the company closed its doors. Beginning in the 1930s, an emerging fad of throwing pie tins, cake pans, and metal can lids took flight in pockets across America. What these chuckers of heavy metal called their games elsewhere in the United States is anyone's guess, but in New England it was called Frisbying, Frisbeeing, Frizbeying, or some other variation on the spelling. When WHAM-O's Pluto Platter began to soar at colleges like Princeton, Yale, and Amherst, the students kept the name they already knew. An article in the May 13, 1957, edition of *Sports Illustrated* confirms this. Titled "Flying Frisbees," it reads, "The air is filled

GAMES ARE FUN
Wham-O Mfg. Co. San Gabriel, Calif.
New gyroscopic airfoil really sails–FUN! FUN!
FRISBEE
WHAM-O®
PLUTO-PLATTER
SKILL
GAME
FLYING SAUCER
UNBREAKABLE POLYETHYLENE SOFT-SAFE
SKIPS
BOOMERANGS
CURVES LEFT OR RIGHT
FLIES STRAIGHT

lately with flying objects, every one of which can be identified as a Pluto Platter by Wham-O. The undergraduates ignore the official name, though, and call the curious gadgets Frisbees."

Adopting the age-old business practice of *if you can't beat 'em, join 'em,* WHAM-O filed for the trademark on the term "Frisbee" two months later in July 1958. "I changed the name to 'Frisbee' because all the kids up in New England were calling them 'Frisbees,'" Rich said. Yet in the minds of hardcore Frisbee fans, WHAM-O should not have been awarded a trademark on a term that was already in the public domain in 1957.

"I never liked the name *Frisbee,*" Morrison said. "I thought it was stupid. The word 'Frisbee' doesn't describe anything." Despite his disillusionment over the name change, Morrison helped promote the newly named Frisbee Flying Saucer. "During the process of getting the Frisbee going, we were real close," Morrison related. "I spent a lot of time at WHAM-O. I was kind of accepted as one of the family."

Other than Fred Morrison, no one had a bigger impact on Frisbee than Ed Headrick. He was welcomed into the WHAM-O family in 1964 and given the job of promoting the Frisbee Flying Saucer to higher sales (see sidebar, page 89). He created the Official Pro Model to distance the Frisbee from the "toy" or "game" that it had become. The obvious first change was the shape of his new disc. Gone were the cockpit cabin, portholes, and celestial names that were molded into Morrison's original disc. In their place he put a black racing stripe, Olympic rings, and an "official" weight printed on a gold decal. Finally, the names "Pluto Platter" and "Flying Saucer" were dropped. Outer space and UFOs suggested "toy," while these new elements screamed "sport!"

No one could have predicted what would happen over the next ten years. Frisbee didn't become just one sport, but *multiple* sports. Headrick formed the International Frisbee Association for WHAM-O in 1967. Also in 1967, a form of "Frisbee Football," where two teams compete in an area the size of a football field, was being played. The object of the sport, invented by some buddies at a New Jersey high school, was to score by catching a pass in the opponent's end zone. They dubbed it "Ultimate Frisbee." By 1968, Frisbee fans were already playing a golf game (with Hula Hoops as the targets!) in which courses were laid out over varying terrain. It was dubbed "Folf" and "Frisbee Golf." The "interpretive dance" of Frisbee play was something called "Freestyle Frisbee," and probably developed immediately after someone made the first behind-the-back catch. Today these sports have all dropped the Frisbee name and are known simply as Ultimate, Disc Golf, and Freestyle.

The sport(s) of Frisbee grew significantly in the early 1970s. In 1974, the World Frisbee Disc Championships were held before a crowd of fifty thousand in the Rose Bowl in Pasadena. Meanwhile, down at Dodgers Stadium that same year, a 19-year-old named Alex Stein ran out onto the field during a Dodgers/Reds game along with his dog Ashley Whippet and a handful of Frisbees. Alex threw, Ashley Whippet ran, jumped, and caught, and the duo delighted the crowd (and the TV cameras), spawning yet another Frisbee sport. Stein was arrested, but not before Canine Frisbee (now called Disc Dog) was introduced to thousands along with Ashley Whippet, the first Frisbee canine celebrity.

OPPOSITE: Rich, Fred, and Spud, in 1968, the First Family of Frisbee.

BELOW: In 1959, WHAM-O released the Frisbee-like Twirl-a-Plate. Promoting it as a "professional model" and encouraging kids to "invent your own balancing tricks," it used marketing phrases that would one day become familiar to Frisbee fans. In 1968 the product was relaunched as the Whirlee-Twirlee and had morphed into a shape even more reminiscent of the Frisbee.

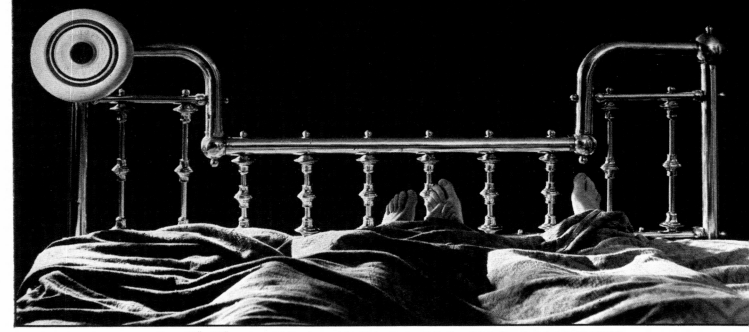

Did you Frisbee today?

If it's not by Wham-o, it's not a Frisbee

For a 23" x 35" poster of this ad, send $1.00 to: Poster, P.O. Box FS-4, San Gabriel, Calif. 91778
Frisbee is a registered trademark of Wham-o Mfg. Co.
for toy flying saucers for toss games

ABOVE: To further establish Frisbee as a sporting-goods item and not a toy, WHAM-O ran suggestive ads like this one, which ran in *Playboy* magazine in 1973.

Yet before all these disc sports, way back in 1958, the Healy Brothers of Michigan invented the game of Guts Frisbee. In Guts, two teams face each other 14 meters apart and try to score points by throwing a disc "in such a manner that the opposing team cannot make a clean catch." In other words, hurling it with all their might. Guts, therefore, is synonymous with the intestinal fortitude it takes to play it.

The invention of Guts, less than a year after the Pluto Platter Flying Saucer was introduced, is a testament to that often-overlooked but crucial power of suggestion molded on the bottom of those first Pluto Platters: PLAY CATCH—INVENT GAMES. Frisbee legend Dan Roddick, the former director of sports promotion at WHAM-O and winner of numerous Frisbee championships, agrees. "It's the nature of disc play, that from the beginning there's been this kind of climate that encouraged people to make

up whatever sport they liked," Roddick said. "My God, over my years at WHAM-O, I bet I had five thousand ideas sent to me, each one called 'The Greatest Frisbee Game Ever.' It seemed to just invite invention. I think because of that, it's pretty hard for Frisbee to get old."

So tight-knit is this legion of disc devotees that the very act of "coming home" is going out to a Frisbee event. "The Frisbee family is a well-known phenomenon," Dan Roddick said. "Someone was coming through town the other day from Denmark and they stayed overnight. We didn't know each other, but an observer would never know that. We talked all evening about common experiences and acquaintances, though we had never met. There are a million stories about players traveling around the world and staying with other Frisbee people and all the shared experiences. I assume that rugby players and dart throwers have similar communities, but I've never run across anything that has the sociology of Frisbee."

The more "Frisbee people" I spoke to, the more the Frisbee family came up. "I'm headed to Arizona tomorrow," Disc Dog competitor Tom Wehrli said. "There'll be people there from Europe. We were in Korea last week. We were in Amsterdam in May. I've been to Japan twice, and all because of this piece of plastic. I know people that have met their spouses, married, had kids—all because of Frisbee events." For Wehrli and other Disc Dog competitors, their canine partners are family. "Do you have any idea how many dogs Frisbee has saved? All these dogs were sitting in shelters, and along comes someone into Frisbee and they get these cattle dogs and border collies and take them out to play."

As more Frisbee sports were invented, more connections were made. Double Disc Court, Discathon, and Gollum were just a few of the disc sports that welcomed more players into the Frisbee family. And if the professional ranks of Frisbeedom warrant this many sports and disciplines, imagine the incredible number of casual Frisbee fans out there, just

LEFT TOP: Comin' at ya! Guts competitor John Begoske lets one loose at the 2006 Guts U.S. Nationals. The Guts Players Association was formed in the late '70s.

LEFT BOTTOM: The Babe Ruth of the sport Disc Dog is Ashley Whippet, shown here, in 1976, flying high above a down-to-earth dog. He has an international Disc Dog tournament and a Disc Dog museum named after him.

Frisbee® flying disc
at the Rose Bowl . . .
Our annual World Frisbee disc Championships put some talented salesmen at your side!

Throughout the year, local Frisbee disc National Series Meets are held all over the United States. Thousands of Frisbee disc enthusiasts test their skills, individually and in teams, for the right to compete in the Annual World Frisbee disc Championships. And they stir up plenty of community excitement as Frisbee discs fly in events like Maximum Time Aloft, Distance, Accuracy, Freestyling and Disc Golf. Team games include Guts and Ultimate. The World Frisbee disc Championships are a part of the great promotional effort Wham-O puts behind Frisbee flying disc to constantly create new interest in the Frisbee disc . . and new customers for Frisbee flying disc dealers.

LEFT: The World Frisbee Disc Championships at the Rose Bowl in Pasadena took center stage in this spread from WHAM-O's 1978 catalog. Note that Freestyle, Ultimate, Disc Golf, Disc Dog, and Guts are all showcased. A year later, WHAM-O sponsored a $50,000 Frisbee Disc Golf Tournament. Frisbee was soaring.

RIGHT: Tom Wehrli plays catch with his dog, Murray, whom he rescued from a shelter. "Murray was two days away from being destroyed," Wehrli said. "Frisbee saved him."

FAR RIGHT: There's more truth in this ad from 1983 than the sexual overtones imply. Frisbee connects people.

OPPOSITE LEFT: "Steady" Ed Headrick, 1924–2002.

OPPOSITE RIGHT: Headrick's marriage in 1978 and his death in 2002 were both commemorated in disc form.

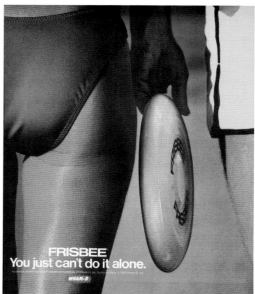

FRISBEE
You just can't do it alone.

throwing it in the backyard or at the beach. It's the casual fan discovering Frisbee that excites Dan Roddick. "Say you've got twenty CEOs in a 40-foot-by-40-foot ballroom at a hotel. What can you do? I'll give you a Gollum tournament that they'll go crazy for. But if you tell me you've got four hundred and fifty Cub Scouts and 2½ acres of undulating farm terrain, then we'll play World War Free. Two guys and a disc and almost any terrain and we'll play Disc Golf. Sure, it's fun to play on a well-designed Disc Golf course, but it's not completely clear that that's more fun than playing down the Appalachian Trail. It's that adaptability. The different contexts are really amazing."

It soars, spins, skips, and sails. It flips, floats, flutters, and flies. Above all else, a Frisbee connects—friend to friend, friend to stranger, people to their pets, and more. For over a half century this simple, round piece of plastic has brought us together. With over 200 million sold all over the world, it's easy to see why Frisbee has become a family affair on a global scale.

The Lines of Headrick
Memorial Freestyle Disc

June 28, 1924
to
August 12, 2002

Herein lie
the ashes of
"Steady" Ed
founding father of
Frisbee and the
sport of Disc Golf.

A Giant of a man
who was many
things to many
people

Fly Free and rest in peace.

ED HEADRICK, who earned his nickname "Steady" from the accuracy with which he threw a Frisbee, worked for WHAM-O from 1964 to 1975. In 1976, he patented what has become the standard disc catcher for the sport of Disc Golf, a sport he helped formalize and promoted throughout his life. He founded the Disc Golf Association (now known as the Professional Disc Golf Association) that same year. Headrick had a hand in the success of many WHAM-O toys, but none more than Frisbee. In 1964 he took a child's toy, a "flying saucer," and turned it into a sport by creating the Official Pro Model Frisbee, which included ridges on the upper surface of the disc. They improved the disc's flight and would become known as the "Lines of Headrick." After leaving WHAM-O to promote Disc Golf, Headrick oversaw the construction of eight hundred disc golf courses in twenty countries. When he married in 1978, his wedding announcement was a plastic flying disc. When Kransco bought WHAM-O in 1982, Headrick's International Frisbee Association was shut down. It had grown to 112,000 members in thirty countries. His obituary in the *San Francisco Chronicle* read, "Just before he died, the man who made the Frisbee soar and who was called the father of Disc Golf said he wanted his ashes to be mixed into new copies of the famous plastic flying disc." His family and the PDGA made "Steady Ed's" last wish a reality with a plastic disc whose surface is printed with the gold words, "Herein lie the ashes of 'Steady' Ed, founding father of Frisbee and the sport of Disc Golf." And not far from the Lines of Headrick he made famous were printed the final words, "*Fly Free and rest in peace.*"

See who can keep their
WHAM-O BIRD up in the air
the longest. Time it with the
second hand on your watch.

7

WINGS 'N' WHEELS

There's something about flying—in the air or over the ground—that thrills every kid. For some it's the speed, others the fantasy of travel, and many the thrill of the ride. For simple purists, there's the danger of a good old-fashioned projectile. WHAM-O gave us all of the above and more.

WHAM-O's foray into vehicles came with the X-15 Space Plane, named after a real rocket-powered experimental plane that became the first winged aircraft to break the sound barrier in the early '60s. It wasn't a rocket but a rubber band that sent WHAM-O's version supersonic. The wings on the X-15 folded flat against the plane's body so that when kids used a stick attached to a long rubber band to shoot the plane into the air (like a rock from WHAM-O's famous slingshot), the wings of the plane remained hidden until the wind resistance let up. Then, "Suddenly—Pop! Out go the automatic wings." The TV commercial promised, "It speeds back to you for a beautiful landing."

electric MONORAIL

HO GAUGE....SCALED SPEED OF 200 MPH

2 GIANT *Deluxe* LAYOUTS

Amazing New Invention
40 foot flexible aerial track!
15 foot steel floor track layout.

BEAUTIFUL STEEL TRACK LAYOUT

OUTDOOR FUN!

New Invention FLEXIBLE AERIAL TRACK

LEFT: At $12.95, the X-20 Monorail was one of WHAM-O's more expensive toys from the early 1960s.

FUN FOR EVERYONE!

...thrilling speeds on single rail!

Carries secret messages to neighbor's house!

Travels long distances!

SAFE !

TTERY OPERATED

DELUXE SET INCLUDES:

- Self propelled monorail engine
- 40 ft. flexible aerial track with curve support
- 15 feet of monorail track
- 10 monorail suspension towers
- 10 horizontal support clips
- 10 suspension tower bases
- 1 variable speed control tower

STOCK NO. 245
PACKED 6 TO A CARTON
WEIGHT 30½-LBS.

$12⁹⁵

COPYRIGHT 1962 **WHAM-O MFG. CO.,** 835 E. EL MONTE ST., SAN GABRIEL, CALIF.

ABOVE: Aqua Jet, released in 1962, offered controlled landings and take-offs at the turn of a faucet.

OPPOSITE: The TV ad for the WHAM-O Tank shouted, "You, too, can have your own tank!" When the cardboard tube was turned on its end, the "tank" became a "fort." Being made of cardboard instead of metal, many a war was probably canceled due to rain.

What the X-15 lacked in reliable returns, the X-20 Monorail had in spades. Released in 1962, the X-20 was likely inspired by Disneyland's monorail, which had debuted three years prior, becoming the first operating monorail in the United States. WHAM-O's version was a fully functioning electric monorail, and a pretty cool toy in its heyday, limited in distance traveled only by the 40 feet of aerial track that came with it.

In contrast, a vehicle that could only go so far was the Aqua Jet, which traveled in a 12-foot circle. Powered by "water pressure from your garden hose," this toy plane turned your faucet into a throttle and made a game of groundskeeping. The TV ads promoted the fact that "It can even water your lawn!"

In 2005, the National Toy Hall of Fame inducted the cardboard box into its hallowed halls. Countless kids will recall playing with the occasional large appliance box their parents brought home and heartily endorse the Hall's decision. If you count yourself among them, then you would have loved the WHAM-O Tank from 1959.

The WHAM-O Tank was an 8-foot-long cardboard tube that a kid could "drive" by climbing inside and crawling. The flexible "track" would travel around the crawling kid like an exercise wheel for a hamster. Released in an era when war toys were prevalent, the WHAM-O Tank came with a helmet, goggles, and an automatic submachine gun. The TV ad encouraged kids to ". . . have modern war maneuvers just like the army."

ABOVE LEFT: The TV ad for the Circus Cycle made it sound easier to ride than it really was. "Just hop on and away you go, faster and faster. Race! Do tricks! Ride to school on your Circus Cycle!"

ABOVE RIGHT: If the Circus Cycle wasn't enough Big Top craziness for you, then you could always bring "a circus right into your home" with the dizzying Tilt N' Whirl.

It's hard to imagine a toy called the Circus Cycle being more dangerous than a "tank with a submachine gun," but it's true. While playing war was all make-believe, this crazy contraption could crack your head open faster than you could say "Circus Cycle" three times fast, which the TV ad did in ridiculous fashion. "All your friends will want to ride your Circus Cycle, Circus Cycle, Circus Cycle!" You were basically asked to balance on a set of metal steps attached to round wooden wheels. You were low to the ground, which helped, but one look at the kids struggling to ride it and keep their balance in the old TV ads was enough to convince me that many a circus fall was had on the Circus Cycle.

Like its Shrink Machine (see page 135), which preceded the successful Shrinky Dinks, WHAM-O was ahead of its time with the Tilt N' Whirl. The fun was very similar to Playskool's Sit 'N Spin, which was released in the 1970s to great success.

Similar to the high-flying X-15 Space Plane before it, the WHAM-O Bird used a rubber band to propel its flight, not by pulling and stretching but by turning and twisting. The uncoiling of the rubber band turned the levers and flapped the wings in a frantic fashion. When you wound it up and let it loose inside your house it looked and acted just like a real bird, flying into the ceiling and all four walls in a desperate shot at freedom. Thankfully the WHAM-O Bird was "practically indestructible," just as the TV ads promised in 1962: "Made with aircraft aluminum and new, super strong Mylar, it won't break no matter what it flies into." Perhaps that was true, but the promise that it "obeys your every command" was over the top, even by WHAM-O's standards.

If *we* had obeyed the every command of our mothers, we would have never popped wheelies on our bicycles. "You'll flip backwards and crack your head open," they all said. What would have saved my mom from years of worry was the WHAM-O Wheelie-Bar from 1966. Modeled after the same design concept that kept dragsters from flipping backward, these "precision-engineered permanent accessories" were attached to the back wheel of your bike. When you yanked your front wheel off the ground, the Wheelie-Bar not only prevented you from falling backward, but it balanced you so that a semi-permanent wheelie was easy.

Children of the '70s were too young to have had a Wheelie-Bar (1966) and too old to have a Roller Racer (1983). Unfortunately they missed two great WHAM-O rides. While the Wheelie-Bar balanced you up in the air, the Roller Racer got you low to the ground where the sense of speed was heightened.

Using the same roller skate–type wheels they used in the Wheelie-Bar, WHAM-O created a vehicle that looked like a cross between a bicycle and a skateboard. You sat on the molded plastic seat with your feet on the handlebars and snaked your way along by leaning and turning the handlebars. Downhill driveways and streets were the best Roller Racer tracks.

BELOW (TOP): The summer of '66 meant barefoot bicycling, banana seats, monkey handlebars, and Wheelies!

BELOW (BOTTOM): A very desirable piece of 1960s Americana, the WHAM-O Wheelie-Bar appeals not only to WHAM-O collectors, but also to bicycle enthusiasts and fans of Ed "Big Daddy" Roth, the cartoonist whose irreverent Rat Fink character decked out the box in 1966. It can sell for over $1,000 in its original box.

Around the same time that Roller Racer was gliding on streets, Morey Boogie boards were skimming across waves on beaches everywhere. Boogie boards, bodyboards, and skimboards have grown within WHAM-O's line since the Kransco Era (see chapter twelve, "What's Next?").

WHAM-O offered speed and thrills with a "WHAM-O!" style throughout the past sixty years. Its ride-on toys transported us farther than the mere distance we traveled on them, while its other wheeled and winged creations thrilled us in different ways. WHAM-O moved us.

ABOVE: Roller Racer rocked . . . literally. That's how you generated forward motion on a flat surface, by turning the handlebars while rocking side to side.

OPPOSITE: Note that Rat Fink is dumping WHAM-O SuperBalls off the back of his ride, something Rich and Spud liked to do, too.

PAGES 100–101: The WHAM-O Bird was one WHAM-O toy that really worked well.

S BY FLAPPING WINGS!

Made of **DU PONT MYLAR***
The new tough-like-steel plastic
with aircraft aluminum spars.

8

MORE FUN THAN EVER!
and
twice as BIG! **2 for $1⁰⁰**

Water Fun

Thanks to WHAM-O, we had all kinds of wacky ways to get wet, from a Water Wiggle and a Water Wiennie to Water Bugs and Big Wheel car washes. In many ways WHAM-O's water toys defined summer silliness. But the company also gave us less frantic fun—a calmer combination of water and soap: the basic bubble. So whether you favor your fun wet 'n' wild or like the beauty of bubbles better, this is the chapter for you.

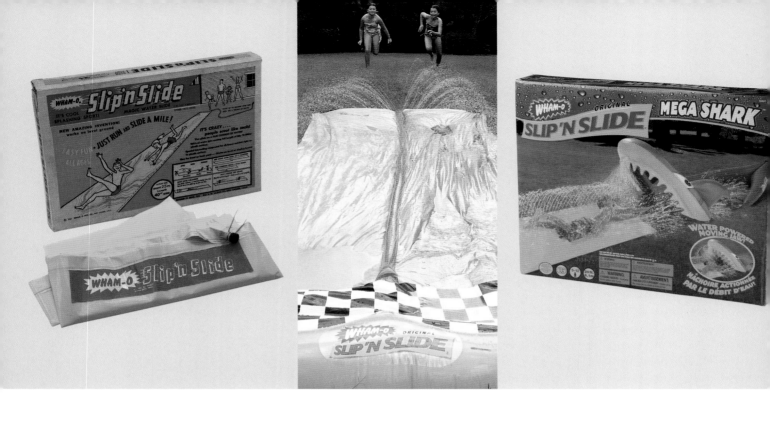

PAGE 102: Water Wiggle had a single tooth and a single aim: Get kids wet!

ABOVE LEFT: Slip 'n Slide, WHAM-O's first water-toy hit was the invention of upholsterer Robert Carrier and came out in 1961.

ABOVE CENTER & RIGHT: Modern Slip 'n Slides feature a pool of water at the end, and often have elaborate inflatable parts like the Slip 'n Slide Mega Shark. The dual model is called the Double Auto Racer.

OPPOSITE: This ad from 1973 shows how Slip 'n Slide evolved from a "Magic" water slide to a "Lawn" water slide.

Summers were changed forever when upholsterer Robert Carrier invented his "Aquatic Play Equipment" (as his patent called it). After watching his son hose down their slick concrete driveway and slide down it like an otter at Sea World, Carrier brought home a long roll of Naugahyde (a tough, vinyl-coated fabric) and set out to give his son a safer surface on which to slide. First he sewed a tube along the edge of a long strip of the sturdy fabric. One end of the tube he attached to a garden hose and the other end he sewed shut. He spaced his stitches along the tube so that when the hose was turned on, water was forced out between the stitches down the length of the tube. This lubricated the vinyl surface and . . . *voilà*! Backyard water slide!

Carrier pitched it to WHAM-O, but the fun of his newly christened "Slip 'n Slide" was something that had to be seen to be believed. "We went over to his house," Rich Knerr said. "He had kids sliding on it in his front yard. It was great!" A deal was struck, and the Slip 'n Slide Magic Water Slide met the world.

WHAM-O modified Carrier's invention to make it affordable, constructing it from thick plastic. Printed boldly on the box top were the words, "Just run and slide a mile." Okay, it was just 25 feet, but the advice proved true. For summer fun, all you had to do was follow the yellow, slick road. The resulting backyard belly flops made Slip 'n Slide a summer staple, and from 1961 through 1992 an estimated 9 million Slip 'n Slide water slides were sold.

Slip 'n Slide®
LAWN WATER SLIDE

Bright, contemporary packaging emphasizes 25-foot lawn slide.

Connect it to a hose, and glide on the cushion of water.

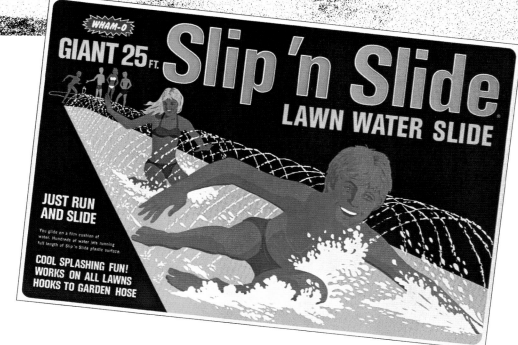

WHAM-O

GIANT 25 FT. Slip 'n Slide®
LAWN WATER SLIDE

JUST RUN AND SLIDE

You glide on a film cushion of water. Hundreds of water jets running full length of Slip 'n Slide plastic surface.

**COOL SPLASHING FUN!
WORKS ON ALL LAWNS
HOOKS TO GARDEN HOSE**

OPPOSITE: Water Wiggle's packaging changed every few years, but the fun never did. Clockwise from top left, the toy in 1971, 1973, 1977, and 1985.

BELOW: Spud Melin filed the patent on his "jet-propelled toy" on June 1, 1962, appropriately enough at the beginning of summer. Water Wiggle became "the laugh miracle of '62."

PAGE 108: Water Wiggle demonstrates its ability to dramatically drench in this publicity photo from 1962.

PAGE 109 (LEFT, TOP AND BOTTOM): Water Wiggle's success spawned a flood of WHAM-O water sprinklers, including Fun Fountain (1979) and Willy Water Bug (1981).

PAGE 109 (RIGHT): Not quite a water balloon and not quite a water gun, the Water Wiennie almost made the Weirdos chapter of this book as one of those "so dumb, it's great" WHAM-O oddities.

Slip 'n Slide titles through the years included a Super Slip 'n Slide, Slip 'n Splash, White Water Rapids, Fast Track Racers, and Wet Banana. When several adults sustained serious injuries using Slip 'n Slide in the early 1990s it was marketed for kids only. Today, inflatable elements have taken the previously flat water slides to incredible 3-D proportions. WHAM-O's Slip 'n Slide Splash Tunnel Pirate Ship is 23 feet long and 12 feet high!

The original Slip 'n Slide was so successful in 1961 that WHAM-O immediately invented other water toys that utilized the ubiquitous household garden hose. The result was Aqua Jet (see page 94), a toy that never took off in popularity, and the much more successful Water Wiggle.

Water Wiggle had a mischievous personality from the very beginning. The water toy narrates its first TV ad: "I look alive. Now let's play tag. Try to get away. You better watch out—I'll catch you every time." Then in the '80s, a chorus of kids sang, "Crazy Water Wiggle, you can't tell what he'll do. You think you're chasing him, then—BOOM!—he's chasing you!"

WHAM-O

WATER WIGGLE

WILD ACTION WATER HOSE

Cool Splashing Fun!

WHAM-O

Water Wiggle®

COOL SPLASHING FUN!

Kids Love it

HOOK
TO HOSE

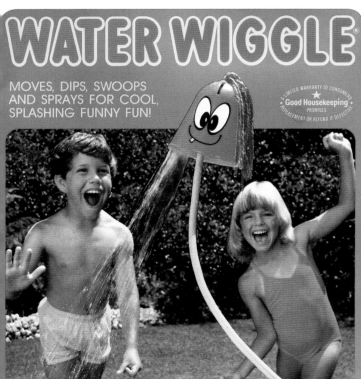

WATER WIGGLE®

MOVES, DIPS, SWOOPS AND SPRAYS FOR COOL, SPLASHING FUNNY FUN!

A LIMITED WARRANTY TO CONSUMER

★
Good Housekeeping
PROMISES
REPLACEMENT OR REFUND IF DEFECTIVE

WHAM-O

Water Wiggle

COOL SPLASHING FUN!
KIDS LOVE IT!

Fun Fountain.
Surprising Action! Cool, Splashing Super Water Fun!

Turn on the water and the hat whirls up .. balancing high atop a cool, splashing Fun Fountain!

Colorful, appealing Fun Fountain is super, summer water fun for all kids from 5 on up. Hat rises to heights of 15 feet (depending on water pressure and wind conditions). Great for water games . . . great for watering the lawn.

Attaches easily to the garden hose. Carefully engineered out of high quality polyethylene (hat) and high impact styrene (clown head) for durability and lasting qualities.

Willy Water Bug™
Super spraying action for cool water fun!

The tubes in the hat lift, move and spray swirling streams of water for cool, funny water play.

Willy's adorable appearance makes him instantly appealing to any youngster. He's carefully engineered and sturdily constructed out of high-quality plastic.

Willy attaches easily to the garden hose and operates perfectly even in low-pressure areas.

Advertised on National TV

DO NOT SQUIRT AT CLOSE RANGE.

ABOVE (RIGHT AND LEFT): James Bond meets the Beatles' *Yellow Submarine* in Pocket Bubbles, WHAM-O's first bubble toy, released in 1963.

OPPOSITE: "Just wave the wand . . . they wiggle 'n' wobble."

Bubble blowing has been around as long as soap, with many companies selling pipes and wands well before World War II. But that didn't stop WHAM-O from adding some wackiness to the bubble toys in 1963, when it released Pocket Bubbles. A clandestine, miniature bubble machine that kids could carry in their pockets, this little toy was "secret" in an era when James Bond and spy toys ruled.

Moving from one end of the spectrum (pocket bubbles) to the other, WHAM-O next gave us bubbles so big the word "giant" was not sufficient to describe them. Released in 1964, Giant Monster Bubbles consisted of a shallow pan that kids filled with bubble solution (WHAM-O included its own generic solution and also recommended several brand-name ones), and a large wand. Instead of blowing them, these huge bubbles were created by dipping the wand in the solution and then waving it through the air right out of the pan.

Sure, other companies also made bubble toys that promised big bubbles, but WHAM-O had a knack for making its toys sound better than anyone else's. Giant Monster Bubbles weren't just big; they were "3- to 6-foot" bubbles! And they didn't just float above the ground; they floated "over houses!"

AMAZING GIANT SIZE BUBBLES 3 TO 6 FT.!

Floats over houses—wobbles and
wiggles. Just wave wand for
exciting action, fun!

We recommend WONDER SOAP BUBBLES, U-BLOW-IT,
or PLAY-TIME SOAP BUBBLES for use with MONSTER BUBBLES.

257	SPECIFICATIONS
Packed 48 per display carton	
Weight: 32 lbs. per carton	

256	Packed 24 per carton
Refill or rack weight 14 lbs. 12 ozs.	

**STOCK
No. 257**

Copyright 1964 **WHAM-O MFG. CO.,** 835 E. El Monte St., San Gabriel, Calif. 91776

In 1963, WHAM-O introduced its Air Blaster toy (see chapter nine, "Back of the Comic Book,"). Perhaps inspired by their own TV commercial, which showed how a ball of air from the Air Blaster could pop a soap bubble, Rich and Spud created an Air Blaster spin-off for their growing bubble line. The Zap-A-Bubble was released in 1968.

Less than a year later, Rich Knerr filed a patent on his "bubble maker" that emphasized quantity over size: Zillion Bubbles. "The first bubble wands made a few bubbles. This made a lot of them!" Rich said.

WHAM-O was great at giving kids everything they could possibly ask for in an inexpensive toy. The "Super Toys" chapter covers the Super Foam Machine from 1968, which produced mass quantities of tiny bubbles. Could WHAM-O possibly go to the extreme in the opposite direction? Could it make a toy that made even bigger bubbles than Giant Monster Bubbles? Impossible, you say? Not for WHAM-O.

OPPOSITE AND LEFT: Supply meets demand in these photographs from 1964. Giant Monster Bubbles get packaged in WHAM-O's San Gabriel, California, production facility and are shipped out to stores the same day.

ZAP-A-BUBBLE ™·

**Kids love to
blow bubbles...
and
Zap 'em**
with
Wham-o's NEW
ZAP-A-BUBBLE
GUN

OPPOSITE: What do you get when you cross a bubble toy with WHAM-O's Air Blaster? Dip, Blow, Aim, Shoot . . . Zap-A-Bubble.

LEFT: The sheer joy on the cartoon kids' faces on this 1966 toy is awesome. The ad copy for the product doesn't hurt, either: "New multi-bubble wand creates zillions of luminescent, shimmering bubbles in every sweep."

RIGHT: By 1970, Giant Monster Bubbles had become just Monster Bubbles, but what it lost in title, it more than gained in value as its partner in suds, Zillion Bubbles, was packaged alongside it to create "Two toys in one!"

Harvard graduate David Stein invented Bubble Thing for his daughter, applying for a patent on the toy in 1985. The patent granted in 1987 describes an apparatus for "Forming and Controlling Large-Volume Bubbles." It's a 20-inch-long wand with a sliding "loop ring sleeve" that allows kids to open and close the space where the bubble is made. This is key to making really big bubbles, because unless there's a way to allow the bubbles to form (i.e., close), all you get are long tubes that break as soon as they leave the wand. The other genius part of Bubble Thing is the "bubble-forming loop," which is made of fabric, or as the patent identifies it, "a flexible, large-pore (substantially noncapillary) material able to store large quantities of bubble solution . . ." All this legalese means nothing to a kid. The burden of proof is in the bubbles. The patent for Bubble Thing promised 8-foot bubbles and it delivers.

Bubble toys have not been in WHAM-O's line for some time, as competitors made cheaper versions of the toys and eroded WHAM-O's market share. No matter. For today's kids who know nothing of WHAM-O's history with Hula Hoop or perhaps even Frisbee, WHAM-O is, and always has been, a water-toy company. As the Slip 'n Slide brand of water slides continues to be the company's biggest seller, WHAM-O will forever remain the coolest company for cooling off.

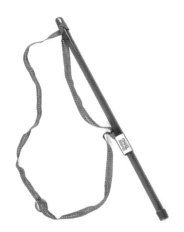

BELOW: WHAM-O topped itself with a "thing" that could make bubbles even bigger than its Giant Monster Bubbles. Bubble Thing was released in 1988.

9

BACK OF THE COMIC BOOK

Fun -- Skill -- Action

In the 1960s, the advertisements in the back pages of comic books were as mind-blowing as the heroics in the front. Sure, you could read about Superman's X-Ray vision in the story, but flip to the back, and you could buy a pair of X-Ray Spex! You could read about Aquaman talking to fish, or turn to the ads in the back to own an instant sea pet that you could train to do tricks! Comic books gave us Sea-Monkeys (not really monkeys), Squirrel Monkeys (*real* monkeys), 100 Toy Soldiers for a $1, and more. WHAM-O didn't advertise in comics often, but this chapter celebrates those WHAM-O toys that *could have* joined Mexican Jumping Beans, hypno-rings, magic tricks, and other oddities we find in the musty back pages of old comic books.

Toy ads with a biological bent, like garden seeds that helped you "earn cool prizes," were commonly seen in comic books. In 1959, WHAM-O did more than offer the possibility of a garden. It promised the farm.

Released in a time of exaggerated ad claims, the TV commercial for Fun Farm featured a misleading combination of time-lapse photography (flowers exploding with color) and a voice that said, "Just put a teaspoon of water in each pot of magic mixture, place in the sun, and stand back. In no time at all they pop through the ground and grow like crazy." The wide-eyed kids exclaim, "Wowee!" You just know some real kids watered, stood back, and . . . waited. (These were the same kids that wondered why the ants in their Ant Farm weren't wearing top hats and waving, like in the ads.) Patience paid off with Fun Farm, though, as kids found their fascination with nature growing, along with fruits, vegetables, and "a mystery plant!"

Like Ant Farm, WHAM-O's Cricket House from 1960 had you mail away to get your critters. Your *Free Cricket Certificate* read, "This certificate entitles me to 2 WHAM-O Singing Crickets." Once they arrived in the mail, you put them inside your domed "house." The TV ad went on to describe: "a clear plastic roof keeps them safe . . . you can watch them sing, play, and dance for hours." I wonder if they were "dancing," or more likely, hopping and crashing into their clear plastic confines trying to escape. The Cricket House, like its trapped inhabitants, didn't live to see 1961.

Also in 1960, around the same time that inventor Harold von Braunhut gave the world his Instant Life (renamed Sea-Monkeys in 1962), Spud Melin and Rich Knerr discovered a species of fish whose eggs would lie dormant in dried-up river beds, just like the brine shrimp that von Braunhut had found. "We discovered these little fish in these dried-up pools [in Africa], and they'd come back to life," Rich said. "We brought them back to the States to start selling them [as Instant Fish], but we could never produce the amount that was in demand." Did he think Instant Fish could have been as big as Sea-Monkeys? "Oh, golly, yes. We had millions and millions of dollars' worth of orders, but we couldn't produce them."

OPPOSITE: Twenty real orange trees, lemon trees, vegetables, and flowers made up the WHAM-O Fun Farm from 1959.

LEFT TOP: This poster was produced for retailers to display in their stores and surely exaggerated the size of the plants in WHAM-O's Fun Farm.

LEFT BOTTOM: Cricket envy marked the opening of the TV ad, with a sad, slightly jealous voice asking, "Hey, what's *he* got?" The voice perked up and answered, "It's WHAM-O's Cricket House, with real live singing crickets!"

PAGE 118: The WHAM-O Air Blaster had such a space-age look it was used as a Martian "ray gun" prop in the 1964 sci-fi cult movie *Santa Claus Conquers the Martians*.

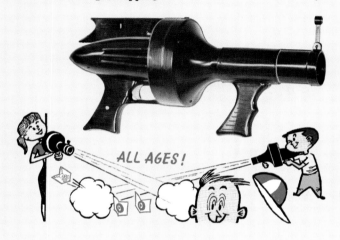

"We got the Fun-Gun from another company that was about to throw it away," Rich Knerr related. "We picked up the parts, took over production of it, and man, that was a great one!" It was renamed and re-released two years later as the classic Air Blaster. When asked why they changed the name, Rich explained, "Well, one name said what it was and the other didn't."

With the Air Blaster's space-age look, the space alien targets make sense, but why the gorilla? Rich responded, "Well, you gotta shoot at something. The ammunition was cheap, too. Free air!"

Rich was quoting the TV commercial, which announced, "Air Blaster shoots air. Powerful, free air!" The patent confirms this: ". . . there is no necessity for recharging the gun at any time since air as ammunition is always present." The Air Blaster worked by a cocking mechanism, activated by a lever on top of the gun, which pulled back on a rubber diaphragm hidden within. When the trigger was pulled, the rubber diaphragm snapped abruptly forward, expelling a blast (actually a ring) of air ahead of it.

When it came to promoting toys, WHAM-O was guilty of its share of hyperbole. When the Air Blaster first came out in 1963, the box top boasted that the gun could shoot a blast of air 40 feet. Twenty feet was probably a more accurate distance, confirmed by the ever-decreasing distance claims for later models of the toy.

WHAM-O

SUPER
AIR ZAPPE[R]
AMAZING

SHOOTS INVISIBLE AIR -15

RIGHT: A miniature version called the Super Air Zapper was released in 1969. A similar model was modified to include a bubble wand so kids could blow bubbles and then "zap" them. WHAM-O called it Zap-A-Bubble (see page 112).

BELOW: WHAM-O originally claimed that the Air Blaster could shoot a blast of air 40 feet. By 1969 it had been reduced to 30 feet, and by 1979 it was simply, "over 18 feet."

JETS A BLAST OF AIR 30 FEET...
safe surprising fun ... action target built into package.

Stock No. 6591
Packed 1 doz. per carton
Size: 22½ x 17¾ x 20⅝
Weight: 21 lbs.

AIR BLASTER ®

'Air Blaster™
Shoots a mysterious ball of air over 18 feet. Packed with its own colorful target.

Here's a surprising, exciting fun for the 5 and over age group. Air Blaster shoots a mysterious, invisible ball of air that can be felt at over 18 feet. Air Blaster is packaged with its own ready-to-use hanging target that "jumps" and reacts whenever the air "bullets" hit. It's super fun . . provides all of the excitement of target shooting without a projectile. Strongly constructed out of high impact materials. Handsomely gift-boxed.

ABOVE: Air Blaster guns get assembled at the WHAM-O production facility in 1964. Just a year after its release, Air Blaster was a hit.

The exotic always intrigued Rich and Spud. They named their early weapons after faraway places, like Borneo, Malaysia, and Africa. So it makes sense that the monster in their Monster Magnet would have a foreign flair, but a genie? He's got pointy ears (with earrings) and a bald head. Perhaps he's a giant, but in that case wouldn't the name Giant Magnet (Monster Strength) be a better name than the chosen Monster Magnet (Giant Strength)? Either way, he's a '60s icon and another WHAM-O winner.

The TV ad for Monster Magnet was nothing compared to the one WHAM-O did for Willie. He was billed as "18" of Flexible Lovable Fun!" but he was nothing more than a pair of jiggle eyes and fabric buckteeth attached to a fuzzy, pipe-cleaner body that could be bent and posed. Yet WHAM-O marketed him as if he were one of the Beatles.

WHAM-O® MONSTER MAGNET
AS SEEN ON TV
GIANT STRENGTH
PRICE $1.49

HAND GRIP

AMAZING POWER
WORKS ON ALL STEEL OBJECTS

FUN! SAFE

..O., 835 E. EL MO..

LEFT: In 1964, common magnets got the monster treatment.

BELOW: The power of Monster Magnet was displayed in WHAM-O's TV ads. Teens played tug of war, hoisted a large Maxwell House coffee can, and even saved a steel toy from the family swimming pool.

ABOVE: Willie had celebrity status in this elaborate TV ad from 1964, where he stars in his own concert, plays guitar, sings, plays bass, dances, cuddles with a coed, plays drums, gets his hair brushed and styled, rides a bike, skateboards, flies on the antenna of a car, and lands on a policeman's night stick. "Here's Willie!"

Willie was positioned as a rock star because his 1964 debut came just as Beatle-mania was gripping the United States. His commercial was one of WHAM-O's best-produced television ads, and certainly one of its most expensive. "Well, that's the way you gotta do it," Rich said matter-of-factly. "Willie was kind of a cute, cuddly toy, and he went over pretty well." The end of the ad tells kids that Willie is "sold everywhere to everyone who wants a fuzzy friend for under $1.00." The fact that WHAM-O could afford a national TV campaign for a toy that retailed for a mere 98 cents tells you just how much television advertising has changed since 1964.

Also retailing for 98 cents was the magic trick novelty called the Nutty Knotter. The object of this odd puzzle was to make a knot appear in the cord "like magic" through a series of single-hand moves made while holding the end of the rope with the wooden knob. Why the other end had a 2-inch-round, fanged-tooth, shrunken head was anyone's guess. It came with a ten-page instruction booklet that started with a basic move and progressed to more advanced tricks. Packaged in a 3-inch tin can, this was another novelty that would have felt right at home in the back pages of old comic books.

From a 3-inch can of tricks in 1966, WHAM-O moved to a nearly 2-foot-tall book of fun in 1967. Rich and Spud liked making their toys giant-size. Over the years they did a Giant Tennis Bird, Giant Tiddly Winks, Giant Hula Hoop, and Giant Monster Bubbles. The last truly giant thing they did, and arguably the most nonsensical, was WHAM-O Giant Comics.

BELOW: In 1966, WHAM-O released this nutty magic trick in a can.

WHAM-O

WHAM-O MANUFACTUR

PHONE AREA CODE 213, CU. 3-1265   835 E. EL MONTE ST • SAN G

We trust by now you have either lost your Super Ball or your male friends will no longer talk to you. Wham-o's Psychiatric Department has developed a new product specifically designed to waste more time than the now infamous Super Ball! So frustrating you can't put it down until you have mastered its strange power. So satisfying it will make you a man among men or women, whatever's right. Bullies will no longer kick sand in your face.

WHAMO'S **NUTTY KNOTTER**, the name was suggested by our Chief Psychiatrist, is specifically intended to free you of inhibitions. However, Group Therapy is sometimes dangerous. We recommend careful attention be paid to the intricately worked out instructions in the tranquil privacy of the executive men's room, or women's room; if the key fits you know you're right. Do not, under any circumstances, permit any juvenile to use your **NUTTY KNOTTER.** The superior attitude of dextrous children is unbearably frustrating.

Gently remove your **NUTTY KNOTTER.** Hold its soft, pliable, friendly head in your left hand, and the carefully worked out instructions in your right hand. If you find this difficult or are left-handed, the procedure may be reversed.

Would you believe a normal mind can master these instructions in 10 minutes? Would you believe 45 minutes? Would you believe we can't figure it out either?

A word of caution — we have found NUTTY KNOTTING so deeply satisfying that prolonged use may cause addiction. If your **NUTTY KNOTTER** is becoming your only passion send $5,296.43 in stamps or coins to Dr. Harry S. Beagle, Psychiatrist, for his 1251 page book, "How I broke the Nutty Knotter Habit" in 1251 easy lessons.

Please accept this gift in the manner in which it was given, begrudgingly — and remember our famous motto, "When **better** toys are built don't blame us."

From the room of
Ed Headrick

Under the care of
Dr. Harry S. Beagle, Psychiatrist

m a n u f a c t u r e r s   o f   n a t i o n a l l y   a d v e r t i s e d   s p o r t i n

WHAM-O Nutty Knotter®
ALMOST... TIES ITSELF!

PRIC
98

HUNTERS DO IT!

SKY DIVERS DO IT

PROFESSORS DO

SURFERS DO IT!

SKIERS DO IT!

EXPLORERS DO

T.M. Reg. & ©1966 Wham-O Mfg. Co.
835 E. El Monte St., San Gabriel, Calif.

Printed in U.S.A.

STOCK No. 282

The inside front cover of WHAM-O Giant Comics offered a fantastic chart of airplanes, or, as the editors put it, a "portfolio of far-out aircraft." The inside back cover featured an article titled "Flying Saucers Mystify the Air Force." Laid out in magazine style, this "story" featured first-hand accounts of UFO sightings and close encounters with alien aircraft. A flying saucer beams up a cow in one panel and shears the wing off a fighter jet in another. In between the covers were "over 1,500 action panels" from a variety of comic book artists like Wallace Wood. There were some funnies, but science fiction dominated the offerings because it was released in 1967, at the height of our space race with the Soviet Union.

OPPOSITE: To promote the Nutty Knotter, WHAM-O sent this letter out to sales representatives. Ed Headrick was WHAM-O's longtime head of research and development (see page 89). This promotional poster went to key retailers.

LEFT: At 14 inches by 21 inches (when closed!), the "World's Largest Comic Book" was a handful even for two kids.

RIGHT: Arguably the best comic within WHAM-O Giant Comics was this full-page look inside the WHAM-O Fun Factory!

OPPOSITE: Shrink Machine was released with a TV campaign starring Professor Shrink, inventor of the "Incredible Shrink Machine." A fun touch was when the Professor said the machine used "Secret Electrotherma Rays," and the words *40-Watt Bulb Not Included* flashed on the screen.

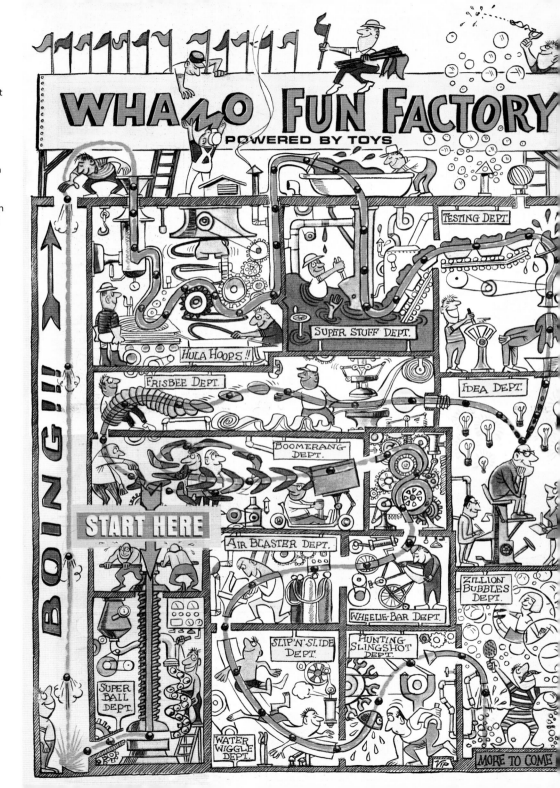

RIGHT: The same year that the foam Nerf Ball rocked the toy world, WHAM-O released its foam ROCK-IT-TO-ME Rocks.

ROCK-IT-TO-ME ROCKS©

from ROWAN & MARTIN'S LAUGH-IN©

Incredibly realistic looking granite rocks out of soft, light-weight foam — in all sizes and shapes

FOR A GIFT...FOR A DECORATION...
FOR THE FUN OF IT!

The Biggest Fad of the Year!

STOCK No. 6763
Packed 3-doz. to the
Counter Display Carton
Size: 17⅝" x 14⅝" x 13⅝"
Weight: 5¼ lbs.

©1969 **WHAM-O MFG. CO.**, San Gabriel, California 91778 · Made and printed in U.S.A.

The copyright notice in WHAM-O's huge comic book stated that it was published, appropriately enough, on April Fool's Day, 1967. It was supposed to come out quarterly thereafter. WHAM-O offered subscriptions and a letter from the editors that urged kids: "Be sure to save this copy! First editions of comic books often become collector's items and very valuable. Ask your store when the next issue of WHAM-O GIANT COMICS will be in!" Another copy never came. Not because of the content, but because of the comical size of the thing! It was just too cumbersome to handle and too "giant" for its own good.

The WHAM-O Fun Factory was at its height in the late 1960s, riding a wave of back-to-back hits with Air Blaster in 1963, Monster Magnet in 1964, SuperBall in 1965, Super Stuff in 1966, and Zillion Bubbles in 1967. In 1968, it *just* missed having another hit with Shrink Machine.

The Shrink Machine came with "Shrinkies" (plastic material kids could color) that reduced in size when heated inside the Shrink Machine. Kids could buy other sets (each sold separately), with names like Tiny-Trinkets, Teeny-Tinys, and Itty-Autos. Yet sometimes being new isn't enough in the business of toys. Timing is another crucial component. The Shrink Machine never caught on in 1968, but it certainly seeded the market for the very successful Shrinky Dinks, which came out four years later, in 1972. And as if misfiring on the timing of Shrink Machine wasn't bad enough, the very next year WHAM-O *almost invented the Nerf Ball!*

Independent inventor Reyn Guyer created the Nerf Ball, which evolved from a game he was developing at the time called Caveman. In Caveman, players hid fake money and hit each other with pretend rocks made of mattress foam. Eventually an "indoor ball" was deemed a better idea, so Guyer ditched the foam rocks and pitched the indoor foam ball to Parker Brothers. Parker Brothers sold 4 million Nerf Balls in 1969, and the rest is toy history. That same year, Rich and Spud, big fans of the hit TV show *Rowan & Martin's Laugh-In*, licensed the rights to produce a toy based on a crazy segment of the show called "Sock It to Me Time." In this segment, a celebrity guest or show regular yelled "Sock it to me!" and then got doused with a bucket of water, walloped with an inflatable mallet, hit with foam rocks, or had some other shocking befuddlement thrust upon them. Rich and Spud liked the foam rocks. The result was WHAM-O's ROCK-IT-TO-ME, "incredible, realistic-looking granite rocks made out of soft, light-weight foam."

Chemistry was a big part of WHAM-O's success, from the polyurethane foam of ROCK-IT-TO-ME Rocks and SuperBall's rubber composition to the balance of the perfect bubble solution, Super Stuff, and SuperElasticBubblePlastic. In 1969 an all-time favorite WHAM-O product was released into the world as a chemical combination of liquid foam resin shot from an aerosol can. You know it as Silly String.

Silly String straddled the same fine line between liquid and solid as WHAM-O's Super Stuff and the classic Silly Putty. It starts as a liquid inside the can, but becomes a continuous solid string of foam outside it. Beyond its obvious fun, a key element to Silly String was that it was just tacky enough to adhere to vertical surfaces, but not so tacky as to stick permanently.

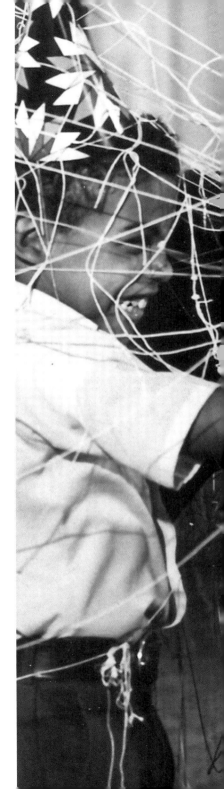

Silly String may not have stuck in WHAM-O's line (the company assigned the trademark to Julius Samann, Ltd, in 1999), but the sticky stuff has endured in other products under a variety of names, including Crazy String, Party String, and most recently in Hasbro's Spider-Man Web Blaster toy. Recent media stories have even reported that Silly String is being used by our troops in Iraq to help detect deadly trip wires that are nearly invisible otherwise. If sprayed into a room (it can shoot up to 12 feet), Silly String is dense enough to hang intact over a trip wire, thus exposing it, but too light to pull the wire to the point of detonation—a not-so-silly use.

In 1971, WHAM-O released a novelty of great renown. If brand extensions are any indication of the popularity of a product, then the Magic Window was pretty popular.

WHAM-O **Magic Window**™

CREATES MOVING, CHANGING PICTURES!

Amazing mystery material makes colorful pictures and designs of flowers, mountains, oceans, etc. **ENDLESS FUN!!**

FLOWERS

MOUNTAINS

OCEANS

DESIGNS

STOCK No. 7501
Packed 12 per Master Carton
Size: 19⅛″ x 13⅝″ x 11 9⁄16″
Weight: 11½ lbs.

FASCINATING "VOLCANIC-ACTION"

©1971 **WHAM-O MFG. CO.,** San Gabriel, Calif. 91778   Made and Printed in U.S.A.

The designs it made could be quite beautiful, but the original packaging of the product reflected the pea-soup green and wood paneling of many a family den in the early 1970s.

The magic within the Magic Window is revealed in its patent. Solid particles (like the grains of sand in Magic Window) have different flow properties depending on their size and shape. Spherical or rounded particles "roll much more easily than cubical particles, which must slide or tumble." Magic Window was filled with two types of colored sand, each with different physical properties, which prevented them from mixing together. Instead, they flowed around each other, creating wonderful patterns.

Magic Window was such a hit in 1973 and 1974 that WHAM-O released an 8-inch-by-10-inch table model and a 3-inch-by-2-inch miniature glow-in-the-dark model dubbed "Glow-show" . . . but it wasn't done yet. The following year WHAM-O produced *three more* versions for its 1975 line. Fluorescent Magic Window glowed in the dark and was marketed almost as a nightlight for kids. ". . . dream a little, watch the pink crystals flow into beautiful fluorescent designs. Take the black out of the darkness." For the artistic desk jockey, there was the Rotating Magic Window "with Decorative Walnut Finished Base." But by far WHAM-O's most ambitious effort was its Magic Window wall decor. It was a full 2-feet-by-2-feet, and came with a ball-bearing wall bracket that allowed you to mount it and rotate it right on your wall!

BELOW: In 1973, WHAM-O released a new version of Magic Window, "Made of Millions of Microdium Crystals."

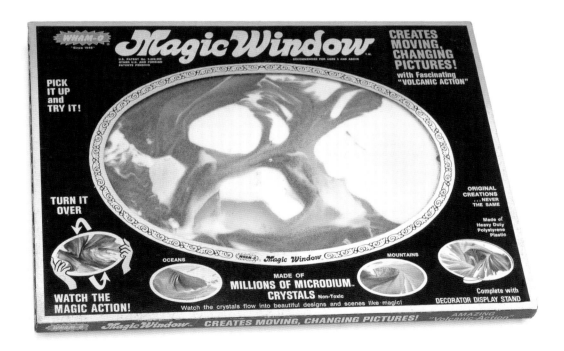

GREAT WHITE

SHARKS TEETH

Craft Kit

MAKE YOUR OWN NECKLACE BRACELET, EARRINGS OR KEY CHAIN WITH GENUINE LEATHER THONG AND CHAIN

From the largest tooth of a Great White Shark taken off the California Coast. This 20 foot man eater weighed over 3000 lbs. Cast in bone like polystyrene, exact in every detail. This species of shark has probably killed more humans than any other shark in the 7 seas. Collectors items and conversation pieces.

KEY CHAIN   NECKLACE   BRACELET

NOW AVAILABLE FOR RACK OR COUNTER DISPLAY. TWO DOZEN PER CARTON WITH DISPLAY CARD.

No. 1452
Packed 12 each
Weight 3 pounds
Carton: 10½ x 9½½ x 6½x

HOBBY CRAFT DIVISION ©1975 WHAM-O MFG. CO., SAN GABRIEL, CALIF. 91778

While Rich and Spud were branching out into home furnishings, they kept their fingers on the pulse of what kids were doing, too, and in the summer of 1975, kids were being terrorized in theaters across the country watching Steven Spielberg's *Jaws*. WHAM-O responded with the Great White Shark's Teeth Craft Kit. (Now that's a mouthful!)

Ever the promoters, Rich and Spud didn't just rely on the popularity of the film to drive sales. "We got possession of a 20-foot Great White Shark that someone caught off the coast," Rich shared. "We promoted that item [Shark's Teeth] for a couple of years. It wasn't a big seller, but we got a lot of publicity out of that shark. We were on TV all the time."

Speaking of TV, the cartoon show *Rocky and His Friends*, and later *The Bullwinkle Show*, aired from 1959 to 1964 and was enjoying renewed popularity in reruns when, in 1972, WHAM-O licensed the rights to make rubber-coated wire toys based on the characters from the series. The wire within them allowed these bendable, "fun-flex" toys to be posed. "We watched TV all the time, looking for what was next," Rich explained.

When you look at the novelties WHAM-O released, the sheer volume of fun is astounding. From A to Z (Air Blaster to Zap-A-Bubble), biology to Bendees, Magic Windows and magic tricks to shark's teeth and Shrink Machines, WHAM-O gave us fun in every conceivable form. "That's a lot of stuff," Rich reflected. "And I bet a lot of it is stuff that people didn't even know we made!"

ABOVE LEFT: Dudley Do-Right and his arch enemy Snidely Whiplash, Mr. Peabody and Sherman, Bullwinkle J. Moose, Rocky the Flying Squirrel, Natasha Fatale and Boris Badenov, were immortalized in flexible rubber in 1972.

ABOVE RIGHT: WHAM-O brought terror to the craft market in 1975, the summer of *Jaws*.

OPPOSITE TOP: It may not have been "the most unique decorative concept of our time," but the Magic Window wall decor weighed 45 pounds and you could give it a spin whenever you wanted.

OPPOSITE BOTTOM: The glow-in-the-dark fluorescent Magic Window was so cool, kids wanted to sleep with it.

WHAM-O®
SUPER SNEAKY

10

SUPER TOYS

WHAM-O toys had great names. Some were long and strange, like the Amazing, Mystical, Mad, Mad Mirror, and others short and punchy, like Slapsie. Often a good adjective was paired with a good noun and . . . presto! Instant Fish! Fun Fountain! Turbo Tops! WHAM-O toys were "Magic," "Silly," and "Giant." But the superlative used to brand no less than eleven of their toys was the word "Super." Most were super, but some . . . not so much.

PAGE 142: He spit like a cobra, but looked like King Kong. He was the 34-inch-long Super Sneaky Squirtin' Stick.

RIGHT AND FAR RIGHT: WHAM-O reintroduced the Super Sneaky Squirtin' Stick in 1977. These catalog shots were accompanied by copy that read, "Just press the head for a long shot of water, just right to catch the kid next door."

The superness began in 1964 with a toy so excellent in its absurdity that it remains an all-time favorite of many a WHAM-O aficionado. The Super Sneaky Squirtin' Stick was a water toy disguised (in super sneaky fashion) as a cane. Kids pulled out the rubber plug and filled the cane with water. When its gorilla head was pressed down, water shot out its mouth like venom. How did it come to be named "Super Sneaky Squirtin' Stick"? "That's just what it was," Rich said. Never mind that there was nothing sneaky about a kid with a cane, or a cane with a gorilla head. Why did Rich and Spud choose to top off the cane with a snarling primate? "For uniqueness," Rich said. "It was a curiosity." Ah—like a plastic flower on the lapel of a prankster clown, this cane would draw an unsuspecting squirtee within range with its "never-before-seen" nature. "What's that? A King Kong cane? Can I take a closer loo—*SQUIRT!* Arghhh! You got me!"

Super Stuff was released in 1966. This product with "1,000s of USES!" arrived from the store as 14 grams of powder, but turned into a half pound of Super Stuff when water was added. The box copy encouraged kids to "drool it" (huh?), "wrap it," "stretch it," "snake it," and even "whip it!"

Super Stuff's elasticity allowed kids to do something they never could with Silly Putty. "Blow Balloons" was the feat that topped the list on the front of the Super Stuff

ABOVE: Super Stuff was made of a "new mystery material" that was gooier than Silly Putty, as this WHAM-O kid from the late '60s discovered.

LEFT: In 1970, New Double Super Stuff was released, with "two fantastic colors!"

BELOW AND RIGHT: Super Stuff didn't come in a plastic egg like Silly Putty, but in a round, plastic tub dubbed a "Stuff Box." Nothing was given an ordinary name by WHAM-O copywriters.

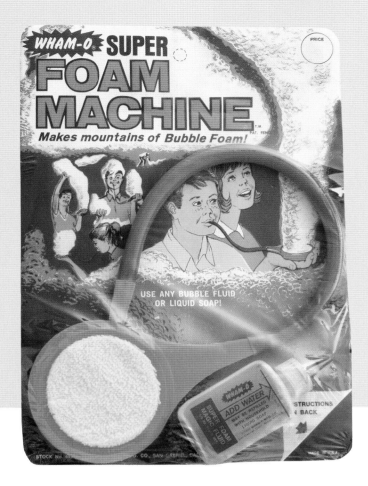

label. But if blowing thousands of little bubbles was more your thing, then WHAM-O's Super Foam Machine was the contraption for you. It was more of a tube attached to a chamber covered with a washcloth than a machine, but it worked pretty well, particularly in the bathtub. It was good to know that once the "Super Foam Magic Fluid" that came with it ran out, you could use "any bubble fluid or liquid soap" to make mounds (if not mountains) of foam.

Why stop at bubbles when you could get freaky and "blow loops of color" with Super-Looper? Spinning a yarn, sure. But blowing yarn? Short lengths worked well, but not the 10-foot-long images of "amazing" looping yarn on the package. Increasing their lung capacity was probably a side benefit as kids tried in vain to make one long loop with one big breath.

WHAM-O's Super-Looper from 1968 should not be confused with its Super Swooper from 1969. Like the X-15 Space Plane that preceded it, the Super Swooper used a stick attached to a long rubber band to launch an aircraft like a slingshot.

ABOVE LEFT: Released in an era that included Candy Cigarettes, the allure of smoking might have been behind this strange "machine" from 1968.

ABOVE RIGHT: This pipe toy wasn't the "Loopin' Fun" the package promised as much as it was just . . . loopy.

RIGHT AND BELOW: WHAM-O's TV ad stated flatly: "It assembles in seconds. It is launched with an incredible device, the rubber band. It can go over 100 feet straight up. It performs an assortment of unbehaveable flight things on its way down. Watch it, if you can. It dips, it loops, it glides, it banks, it swoops. Go on, fly your own UFO. The Super Swooper from WHAM-O!"

OPPOSITE: In the summer of 1970, kids risked inhaling toxic fumes to "blow giant colored plastic balloons!"

WHAM-O **SUPER SWOOPER**

FANTASTIC SPACE AGE FLYING DEVICE ™

Pat. Pending

SHOOTS OVER 100 FEET STRAIGHT UP...

SWOOPS LOOPS and GLIDES DOWN!

2-COMPLETE SUPER SWOOPERS

WHAM-O **SUPER SWOOPER** ™

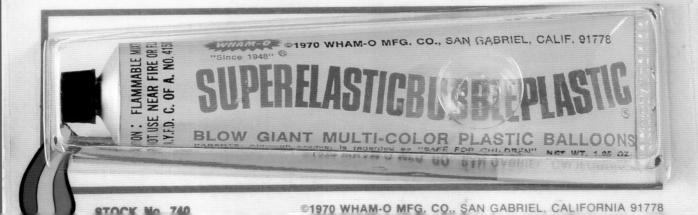

WHAM-O®
SUPERELASTIC-BUBBLEPLASTIC®
Not recommended for children under 5 years old.
Blow Giant Multi-Color Plastic Balloons!

Aircraft? More like "fantastic space-age flying device." The TV ads touted it as a UFO, which stood for an "Unbehaveable Flying Object."

The Super '70s brought with them a legendary WHAM-O product: SuperElasticBubblePlastic. According to Rich Knerr, its funky long name was inspired by "supercalifragilisticexpialidocious," a phrase popularized in Disney's 1964 film, *Mary Poppins.* "My brother was second in command at Walt Disney Studios," Knerr said. "We called it that because it sort of rhymed with that phrase." SuperElasticBubblePlastic. The name says it all.

The packaging read "NOT RECOMMENDED FOR CHILDREN UNDER 5 YEARS OLD," and it also warned, "CAUTION: FLAMMABLE MIXTURE" and "DO NOT CHEW OR SWALLOW" and "NOTE TO PARENTS: KEEP AWAY FROM PAINTED SURFACES AND FURNITURE." SuperElasticBubblePlastic had an air of danger around it and *printed right on it!* It came in a pliable, metal tube, just like your big brother's rubber cement and many other toxic substances—all of which were placed out of reach of small children. Yet you could actually play with this stuff in the bright yellow, metal tube! For many kids, the perceived danger was irresistible.

The fun began when you squeezed out a blob of multicolored plastic on your finger and molded it around one end of the 4-inch tube that came with it. Next, you'd slowly blow into the other end of the tube to inflate. After *carefully* pulling the bubble off and pinching the blowhole shut, you had a semi-permanent bubble of plastic. The stuff was tacky at first, but would dry enough to handle pretty quickly. More than a few kids will recall using up an entire tube making a psychedelic snowman with a swirled bubble body in red, blue, and yellow.

To use the parlance of the times, SuperElasticBubblePlastic was a gas. No, really. Beyond the polyvinyl acetate, pigments, and plastic fortifiers, it contained acetone, the main ingredient in nail polish remover. You had to use your tongue to plug the tube if you were handling the bubble or the air would escape back into your mouth, along with noxious fumes.

OPPOSITE: SuperElasticBubblePlastic fit the '70s like a psychedelic glove. This package is from 1977.

LEFT (TOP AND BOTTOM): SuperElasticBubblePlastic allowed kids to blow bubbles that dried so quickly, they could actually be "handled" and even "stacked."

LEFT (CENTER): WHAM-O's TV ad instructed kids to, "Just squeeze it out and blow them up. They last and last." And float up into trees!

Concerns over safety, coupled with the fact that the stuff was not friendly to the shag carpets common in the 1970s made it a plaything whose days were numbered. SuperElasticBubblePlastic was taken off the market in the 1980s, but the elation of creating "Plastic bubbles from a tube!" was fun while it lasted.

If you wanted more permanent bubbles that were 10 feet long and relatively fume free, you could always go for WHAM-O's Super Balloon. Also released in 1970, it was sold by WHAM-O well into the '80s. Instead of puffing through a straw, this monster was inflated by tying one end of it closed and running with it!

SUPER BALLOON! ®

RECOMMENDED FOR 5 YEARS AND OVER

NT 10-FOOT
LOON
Y TO INFLATE

foreign patents pending.

®Super Balloon! is a brand name and a registered trademark of Wham-O Mfa. Co

WHAM-O

Super Balloon

AMAZING SIZE!

SAILS OVER 100 FEET!

STOCK No. 4782
Packed 24 per Carton
Size: 14⅛″ x 11¼″ x 9⅝″
Weight: 6 lbs., 10 ozs.

STOCK No. 4786
Packed 72 per Master Carton
Size: 18½″ x 10¾″ x 19″
Weight: 18 lbs., 10 ozs,

GIANT 10 FT. BALLOON

ABOVE: Ten feet of fun from 1970.

LEFT: The rhyming TV ad from 1984 went: "Super Balloon! It's about 10 feet long, and made of a plastic film that's strong. To inflate, run into the wind and then puff. The rubber band goes on when it's filled enough. You can throw it, rebound it. You can kick, spin, or pound it! You can play catch with some friends. Have a big laugh. Or make a giraffe! Super Balloon!"

ABOVE: We conducted our own super experiment and dropped a tennis ball from 6 feet. It bounced ten times for approximately five seconds. An original 1965 Super-Ball, dropped from the same height, bounced seventy-five times and took over thirty seconds to finally come to a stop!

RIGHT: It was made mostly of a synthetic rubber called polybutadiene, but WHAM-O dubbed it "Zectron" when the ball debuted in 1965. To this day, the image of a SuperBall bounding over a suburban home is fixed in the minds of big kids everywhere.

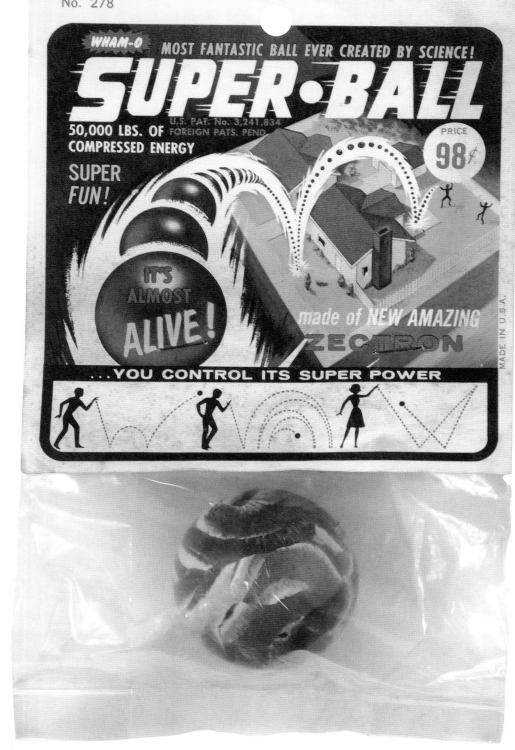

No. 278

WHAM-O MOST FANTASTIC BALL EVER CREATED BY SCIENCE!

SUPER·BALL

U.S. PAT. No. 3,241,834
FOREIGN PATS. PEND.

50,000 LBS. OF COMPRESSED ENERGY

SUPER FUN!

PRICE 98¢

IT'S ALMOST ALIVE!

made of NEW AMAZING ZECTRON

MADE IN U.S.A.

...YOU CONTROL ITS SUPER POWER

Of all WHAM-O's super toys, super contraptions, and super goo, it was a super ball that rose above the rest. WHAM-O's SuperBall came out in 1965, and immediately got noticed by kids and adults alike. No one had seen anything like it. It was hyped as having 92 percent resiliency, which meant that it would bounce back 92 percent of the distance from which it was dropped.

Chemist Norm Stingley invented the SuperBall in an oil company lab and brought it to WHAM-O in 1964. In a meeting at WHAM-O headquarters, Norm lightly bounced the ball once for Spud and then handed it to him. Predictably, Spud bounced it too hard, and the ball hit the ceiling. Melin was impressed, but what really sold him on the ball was something called "The Table Trick." SuperBall had "an extremely high coefficient of friction," which was a scientific way of saying that it would grip a surface. SuperBall would either increase its spin or reverse its spin depending on the surface it hit and the angle at which it hit. In the case of the table trick, the ball would reverse its spin when it met the underside of a table, and send the ball back in the direction from which it came.

The "Table Trick" and drop test were a few of the less violent things kids could do with SuperBall, and early testing at WHAM-O revealed that it would break apart. "We put a lot of development into SuperBall," Rich told me. "Norm would bring some in and they'd break. So I said, 'Back to the drawing board, Norm!' We almost didn't make it."

Stingley added vulcanizing agents and perfected the chemical combination and molding process required to make the ball super. This was no small task. The patent issued in 1966 specified that the time, temperature, and pressure for the molding of SuperBall was 15 to 20 minutes at approximately 320°F and 1,000 pounds per square inch. The result was a ball that could not only bounce over your head, but over your house.

ABOVE: The Firetron from 1970 gave the SuperBall a fluorescent upgrade, and 1976's SuperBall with "Bionic" bounce was meant to capitalize on *The Six Million Dollar Man* TV show. The bounce came back in 1998, when WHAM-O reintroduced the "Original SuperBall." In 2002, Zectron took center stage once again and finally, in 2008, "the ball with the Incredible Super High Bounce" celebrated WHAM-O's 60th Anniversary.

WHAM-O
SUPER·BALL DICE

MADE OF NEW AMAZING ZECTRON

PRICE 98¢

PAT. PEND.

UNBELIEVABLE ACTION!

AMAZING BOUNCE!

MAKES ALL GAMES *MORE LIVELY!*

STOCK No. 298

Made with the same material as Super Ball Balls which are covered by Patent No. 3,241,834

©1966 — WHAM-O MFG. CO., SAN GABRIEL, CALIF. MADE AND PRINTED IN U.S.

Made with the same material as SUPER BALL balls which are covered by Patent No. 3,241,834, additional patent

SUPER·BALL BASEBALL

WHAM-O

AMAZING HOME RUNS!

NEW SUPER-S BALL
U.S. PAT. P

STOCK No. 29:

Made of New SUPER-LITE ZECTRON

MADE AND PRINTED IN U.S.A.   ©1966 WHAM-O MFG. CO., SAN GABRIEL

U.S. PAT. No. 3,241,834   FOREIGN PAT. PEND.

WHAM-O

SUPER·BALL GOLF

wow! What a Ball!

FOR 19th HOLE US ONLY!

Appro 92° REBOU

Made of NEW AMAZING ZECTRON!

50,000 LBS or COMPRESSED ENERGY

Stock No. 296

IT'S ALMOST ALIVE!

©1966 WHAM-O MFG. CO., 835 El Monte Street, San Gabriel, Calif. 91778

Six million SuperBalls were reportedly sold in 1965. A *Life* magazine story from December of that year reported that, "Though you may never have heard of Wham-O before, you doubtless are already acquainted with SuperBall, their latest sensation. . . . Kids from 7 to 70 can be seen dribbling it or whamming it over the rooftops almost anywhere you go these days." WHAM-O extended the line almost immediately to capitalize on its success. In 1966 there were "Mini" Super Balls (3/4-inch diameter) and "Small" Super Balls (1 1/8-inch diameter) to go along with the original 2-inch model. WHAM-O once had a SuperBall formed out of a bowling-ball mold for promotional purposes. "They bounced it in the hallway of a hotel and it broke through a wall," Norm Stingley related. "That was the end of that!" Maybe 2 inches is as big as a SuperBall should be. In another celebrated incident, this giant SuperBall was "accidentally" dropped from a 23rd floor hotel window and bounced back fifteen stories. A tall tale or SuperBall fun fact? No one knows for sure.

There were also other high-bounce balls with names like "Ski-Hi" and "Jet Ball." Between 1965 and 1975, more than 20 million SuperBalls were sold, not including these inferior wannabes. WHAM-O tried to fight them off, going so far as to print a full-page ad in its dealer's catalog that announced the granting of Norm Stingley's patent on the SuperBall (he assigned it to WHAM-O) and the threat to "vigorously enforce this patent against all infringements immediately upon issuance at all levels, manufacturing, wholesale, and retail." But it was too late. It's hard to compete with 25-cent balls available from coin-operated machines outside the doors of every Kmart in the country, and that's exactly what SuperBall's success spawned. With the market saturated, sales dipped, and SuperBall was taken out of the WHAM-O line in 1977.

In the ever-changing retail toy climate of today, phrases like "50,000 pounds of compressed energy!" and "Zectron!" send one right back to the security of childhood. While there are high-bounce balls, bouncy balls, and rubber balls, only one can truly be called "Super." ◆

SUPER MARBLES
MORE FUN THAN ORDINARY MARBLES BECAUSE OF BACKSPIN AND BOUNCE EXPERIMENT!

SMALL PART NOT RECOMMENDED FOR CHILDREN UNDER THREE YEARS OLD

MOST FANTASTIC BALL EVER CREATED BY SCIENCE ! 50,000 LBS OF COMPRESSED ENERGY

HI-BOUNCING BALL

IT'S ALMOST ALIVE!

MADE IN TAIWAN

MOST AMAZING BALL

HI-BOUNCER

FOR ALL GAMES

TRY YOUR SKILL

MARX TOYS

LOUIS MARX & CO., INC.

ENERGY +

ZOOMABALL

49¢

CRAZY SONIC BALL

MADE OF NEW FANTASTIC ELASTON VULCANIZED UNDER 100,000 LBS. PRESSURE!

FLI-BACK

LEFT AND ABOVE: SuperBall's bounding popularity attracted competitors. Marx Toys only imitated the SuperBall with its Hi-Bouncer, but the Hi-Bouncing Ball was a direct rip-off, complete with three of WHAM-O's trademarked Super-Ball slogans. If these balls hurt the market for SuperBall, then the inferior-bouncing Zoomaball killed it by promising twice the compressed energy (100,000 pounds of pressure—it bounces over a three-story building!) and selling for half the price.

11

IT HOPS..IT LEAPS..RUNS
IT'S ALMOST ALIVE..

WEIRDOS

what makes it dart about?

It's a fickle business, the business of toys: Grown-ups trying to figure out what playthings will appeal to children—the ficklest of all consumers. The best toy makers are like Tom Hanks's character in the movie *Big*. He understood what kids wanted because he was a 12-year-old stuck in a man's body. That explains some of the success of Spud Melin and Rich Knerr, two big kids who never left childhood behind. That said, some of WHAM-O's stranger products make you wonder, "What on earth were they thinking?"

PAGE 160: The Amazing Mystical Mad Mad Mirror was half you, half me, and totally freaky.

RIGHT: The TV ad for WHAM-O's short-lived Draw Yarn called it "the latest craze from Europe. Magic Pen draws pictures with real yarn in color. Draw beautiful pictures on easy patterns, ready to frame. You'll love it!" We didn't.

WHAM-O® draw Yarn

STICKS TO MAGIC PAPER

the latest craze from EUROPE!

NEWEST DRAWING FUN — Imagine — draw pictures yarn like you would with pencil or crayon. No mess - fuss! Just follow our patterns to create beautiful pict —even trace pictures from photos or magazines . . . or cr your own. Hours of fun for all ages! Pen uses ordinary

EASY · CREATIVE · FUN

No. 170
Individually boxed
1 Dozen per case
Shipping weight
11 ¼ lbs per Dozen

$2.9

WHAM-O MFG. CO., SAN GABRIEL, CALIFORNIA

Simple easy-to-do designs for beginners, that can be developed into beautiful works of art

© Copyright 1959 Wham-O Mfg. Co., San Gabriel, California

In the previous chapter, a toy called Super-Looper posed the question of why anyone would want to "blow" yarn. Here, we can ask, who would want to draw with it? Europeans, apparently.

Weirdness in its toys began early for WHAM-O. Name changes were common, and whenever a product was rehashed under a new title, it became an "Amazing New Invention!" "WHAM-IT" became the "New Giant Tennis Bird" and then "Big Bird." "Bali-Ball" became "Whing-Ding." "Twirl-A-Plate" was rehashed as "Whirlee Twirlee," and on and on. It was as if WHAM-O's internal product development process was on display within its print ads and on toy store shelves.

"What should we rename this Flyin-Saucer plastic disk we just licensed?"

"How about we call it the 'Pluto Platter'?"

"Let's advertise it as a 'Pluto Platter Flying Saucer' here and 'Pluto Platter Boomerang Saucer' in this ad over here, and then we'll see which one sells the best."

"How about the 'Sputnik Sailing Satellite'?"

"Okay, 'Frisbee' it is!"

WHAM-O
CUTE SCOOT
I'm a new Pet...I'LL LOVE YOU!

Pull Me Back
to have some Fun!
Rubber motor
makes me Run!

ABOVE AND OPPOSITE: Beautiful Caribbean Dancer or Chubby Checker? You decide.

Spud and Rich were not very rigid in their approach to marketing toys, which was one thing that made WHAM-O so great. It also led to many WHAM-O weirdos like the often renamed "Moon Cat." The TV ad let you know that this little pull toy was trouble. "Everyone loves this amazing new pet . . . because everyone likes a fun toy who can run away from you . . ." They do?

A similar renaming occurred with WHAM-O's Limbo Game. Released in 1961 at the beginning of the limbo dance craze, the box top read, "The Caribbean FUN FAD is here!" It came with a 45 rpm limbo record to play with the game—"The Kookie Limbo," by a recording artist named Kookie Joe. Then in 1962, Chubby Checker released a song called "Limbo Rock" (fresh off his mega-hit "The Twist" in '61). Sensing promotional potential, WHAM-O used Chubby's star power to boost sales of its Limbo game. The newly christened Chubby Checker Limbo contained wooden barefoot stands and adjustable dowels to make up a game that provided "A thrill every time." Unfortunately, in the update you still had to settle for Kookie Joe on the 45.

CHUBBY CHECKER*

WHAM-O LIMBO PARTY game

THE DANCE CRAZE THAT'S SWEEPING THE COUNTRY!

Have your own LIMBO PARTY!

The Funny Monster Family

WHAM-O

Beasties

BE A MONSTER MAKER

MAKE 100's OF CREEPY CRAWLERS with this Kit
CREATE YOUR OWN - just push 'em together, take
'em apart - make new ones - QUICK - EASY

A LAUGH A MINUTE!

PUPPETS TOO!

STICKS TO WALLS!

Beasties
ZANY wild
weird

ABOVE: A lightweight challenge to Hasbro's Mr. Potato Head. Despite claiming to be monsters that "would scare Frankenstein," Beasties were more cheap than chilling.

OPPOSITE: Earthmovers didn't move us.

Beasties encouraged kids to play monster-maker to create "100s of creepy crawlers." Released in 1964, the same year that Mr. Potato Head went from vegetable (potato) to mineral (plastic), Beasties briefly battled for shelf space alongside Hasbro's heavy hitter, but ended up being lightweights. That's because they came in a huge, 24-inch-by-12-inch box but weighed less than 2 pounds owing to their cheap Styrofoam body parts. And even though the collection also came with toothpicks, pipe cleaners (called fuzz sticks), construction paper, and stickers, Beasties never lived up to their "laugh a minute" box-top billing.

Also in '64 came Earthmovers. Sort of a miniature sandbox on legs, this play set featured a metal bulldozer and dump truck that kids could move via a magnet they controlled on the underside of the playset. Two types of sand were provided to give some realism and some "earth" for these Earthmovers to push around. With the vehicles seemingly moving by themselves and a large, plastic lid covering everything, Earthmovers was sort of cross between a magic trick and a construction-site terrarium.

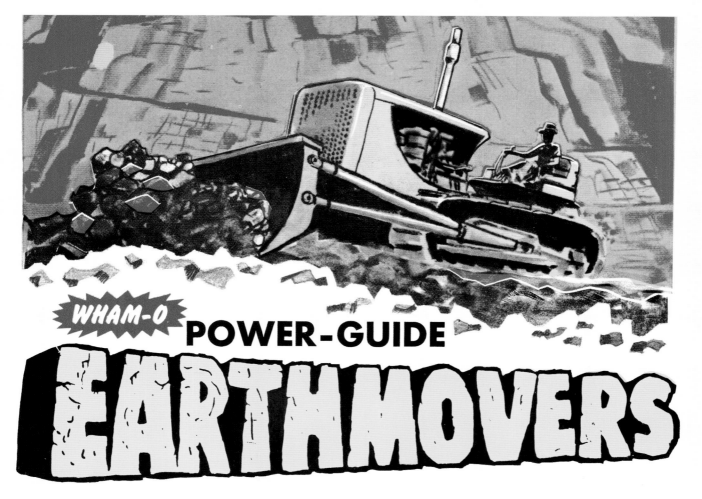

WHAM-O
POWER-GUIDE
EARTHMOVERS

WHAM-O "EARTHMOVER" COMES COMPLETE WITH LARGE MAGNET, FOR
POWER—EARTH MOVING MATERIAL. BULLDOZER AND DUMP TRUCK THAT
ACTUALLY DUMPS AUTOMATICALLY

SPECIFICATIONS
Packed 12 per carton
Weight 16 lbs. per carton

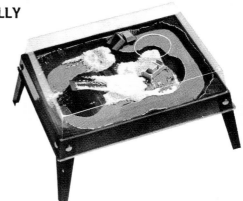

ABOVE LEFT: Never one to ignore a hot trend, WHAM-O leveraged the success of Pillsbury's Funny Face soft-drink mix with its Fun Fountain in 1969.

ABOVE RIGHT: Hard to say what's worse—the theme/name of this game from 1971, or the shirt worn by the teenager on the front of the package.

Pillsbury's Funny Face soft-drink mix found popularity in the wackiness of the mid-1960s. Just like Kool-Aid, you added water to Funny Face packets to make flavors with nutty names like Chug-a-lug Chocolate and Goofy Grape. But what if you could combine flavors to create your own LemonGrapeChocolate concoction? Kids could do just that with WHAM-O's Fun Fountain from 1969. WHAM-O reused the name "Fun Fountain" in 1977, this time on a clown water toy (see page 109). Inspired by Funny Face's success, WHAM-O got into the soft-drink arena in 1969 with a toy/drink mix product called Kooky Froots. Instead of paper packets, this mix came in plastic, fruit-shaped containers that doubled as "toys" after the drinking was done.

Two similar, funkedelic fun things shared space in WHAM-O's 1978 line. Slapsie and Flurry fit the disco era, and yet reminded us of older toys. There was something very *Mork & Mindy* meets Slinky about them both.

Slapsie beats Flurry in this clash of snake-like toys. Slapsie's paddle-like appendages made a delightful clickity sound as it moved, whether it was walking in your hands or paddling down a slanted surface. The appendages pulled apart and snapped back together easily to allow kids some creative choices in their play.

Flurry, on the other hand, was a 5-inch-tall by 3-inch-wide by 3-inch-deep deck of construction paper glued together in accordion-like fashion. Is it a decoration or a toy? A clue comes from the back of the box, which gave "helpful hints" for "top performance," and listed seven Flurry tricks to master, with names like "Fling," "Rippling Rainbow," "Sunrise," "Big Dipper," and "High Fall." Flurry had no ability to recoil on its own, so many of these tricks ended with a "flurry" of twisted paper on the floor. Like a dreaded kink that often spelled the end for a metal Slinky, the nail in Flurry's coffin was a rip across its paper innards.

ABOVE: These similarly psychedelic toys debuted into WHAM-O's 1978 line.

NEW! DIFFERENT! EXCITING!

Magic Sand™

KIDS CAN...draw under water pictures!
Build weird underwater cities!
They can...stack it into towers or pillars
or just make wild, underwater things.
But when it comes out of the water...
Magic Sand is instantly dry! So it can
be used...over and over again.

NEW! WHAM-O

ABOVE AND RIGHT: Magic Sand's science was treating normally absorbent particles with substances that rendered them "hydrophobic."

ABOVE RIGHT: "Mirror, mirror on my table, mix our faces, if you're able." The lens on WHAM-O's Amazing Mystical Mad Mad Mirror was half window/half mirror, and when it spun, it created an often unsettling illusion.

The Amazing Mystical Mad Mad Mirror came out in 1979. When you placed this funky 17-inch-tall contraption between you and a friend, then spun the window/mirror via the battery-operated trigger, it combined your two faces in freaky fashion. The label read, "Press the button and you'll see . . . half you, and half me! . . . Try it at your next party!"

Earlier we pondered the preposterous notion of drawing with yarn. Unbelievably, WHAM-O topped that feat in 1980 when it encouraged kids to draw with sand . . . under water.

Magic Sand wasn't literally "afraid of water" as much as it was repelled by it. When the "sand" was scooped out of the water, it was instantly dry, because it had absorbed no water. The play value was all in Magic Sand's chemistry, but predictably WHAM-O credited a magic genie on the box top.

Like many WHAM-O toys, the company's early '80s tops game underwent a name change. It was called "Knock Yer Top Off!" in 1981 before becoming "Turbo Tops" in 1982. Although the name changed, the design remained the same: powering the tops by blowing through straws. While the air mechanism for spinning these tops worked well, the coolness factor was missing from both versions (it's difficult to look cool with a straw in your mouth), and the game didn't make it to 1983.

What made Spud Melin and Rich Knerr so great at what they did was their willingness to try *anything*. Were many of their flops ridiculous? Yes, but in toys, isn't that part of the fun? Their fearless approach should be celebrated, because without it, we wouldn't have all these wacky (but wonderful) WHAM-O Weirdos.

BELOW: It was perfectly acceptable to blow your top in this WHAM-O game.

years of Fun!

WHAT'S NEXT?

In 1982, after thirty-four years in business together, Rich and Spud decided to sell WHAM-O. A company called Kransco reportedly outbid Hasbro with a buy-out price of $12 million. "We got an offer for the company, and we decided to take it," Rich said. "It was lucrative." In an article for the *Boston Globe*, journalist Joanna Weiss wrote, ". . . Melin, his health declining, decided to sell his shares, and Knerr followed suit." It was a sad day for many inside the Fun Factory.

PAGE 172: To celebrate its 60th anniversary, WHAM-O is releasing this 3-Pack featuring all-time favorites: a Pro Classic Frisbee, an Original SuperBall, and a Hacky Sack footbag.

BELOW RIGHT: To their credit, the new owners of WHAM-O tried to bring back some old-school favorites in 1998, but kids and the toy industry had changed.

"I cried and cried when they told me I had to leave the company," longtime WHAM-O employee Jenny Martinez shared. "WHAM-O was the only place I ever worked. I had everyone crying, because I was crying. It looked like a funeral." Lori Knerr added, "I don't think my dad ever really wanted to sell. He'd still have it today, I think. Those were the best years of his life. Kransco kept him and Spud on for five years as consultants. I think it was just a way to ease the pain."

John Rosekrans and John Bowes founded Kransco in 1963. In buying the rights to Morey Boogie boards around 1978, WHAM-O in 1982, and Power Wheels, a line of motorized miniature ride-on vehicles, in 1984, they were well on their way to becoming the largest privately owned toy company in the United States. With a penchant for acquiring companies, building them up, and reselling them, Kransco's plan with the WHAM-O brands from the start was to eventually sell them. In other words, the family nature of Rich and Spud's WHAM-O was gone.

A year into Kransco's ownership, Hacky Sack footbags were added to the WHAM-O fold (see page 44). Yet, like Frisbee, Hula Hoop, Slip 'n Slide, and other WHAM-O mainstays, Hacky Sack had to get in line when it came to attention from the new owners. The real moneymaker for the company was Power Wheels. Longtime Kransco employee Laura Sciutti witnessed it all. "I went to the Power Wheels plant in Fort Wayne, and it was a mini automotive plant," she recalled. "There were lines and lines of workers building little cars. We even had a list of service centers, like real carmakers. If you had a problem with your Power Wheels car, you could take it to one of these service centers to get it fixed. Power Wheels was where the money was, but the Hula Hoops and Frisbees—that's where all the fun was."

In 1994, Kransco sold its company to Mattel. By most accounts the toy giant purchased the company to get Power Wheels, which today is still a part of its Fisher-Price line. Frisbee, Trac-Ball, and Hula Hoop were folded into a division called Mattel Sports. The WHAM-O name and logo were about to be relegated to the dusty corners of toy history when, in 1997, Mattel sold the WHAM-O trademarks for about $20 million to a group of investors led by the New York–based Charterhouse Group.

In WHAM-O's heyday, Rich and Spud created inexpensive toy and novelty items, many of which "sold for under a dollar!" to "all toy, drug and department stores." They sold to variety stores, mom

Choose Power Wheels® for just one reason.

30 month old Stacy loves to ride in her Camp Barbie ride-on.

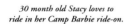

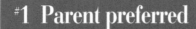

#1 Parent preferred
#1 Kid requested
#1 For 25 years

24 month old Sam loves his Mickey Mobile.

There are a lot of good reasons why Power Wheels® is the #1 battery powered ride-on. First, only Power Wheels has 25 years of experience designing and building literally millions of battery powered ride-ons for kids from 12 months and up. And no one but Power Wheels has an extensive line of 19 models that really excite little imaginations: from our Camp Barbie,™ to the Lil Suzuki® and our popular Mickey Mobile. And parents also love Power Wheels because they're durable enough to last for many years - with easy to recharge batteries, patented safety features and plenty of play value to keep kids busy and happy. Power Wheels models start at just $79 and there's even a toll-free customer number. It all adds up to more miles of smiles for you and your kids - reason enough why we're number one.

For information and a free brochure call
1-800-348-0751

POWER WHEELS.

More Miles of Smiles.

15 month old Andrew gets a big kick out of his Lil Suzuki.

OPPOSITE AND LEFT: Water play and the extension of the Frisbee line continued to dominate WHAM-O's offerings from 2001–2003.

BELOW: The TV commercial that helped launch Frisbee in the late 1950s would never reach the airwaves today because the cost of television advertising has skyrocketed, while its effectiveness has been diluted across hundreds of channels. Add to this the fact that the margin of profitability for traditional toys has diminished, and you have a tough sell for toy makers like WHAM-O.

and pop hardware stores, and five-and-dime stores like Woolworth's, Newberry's, and H. J. Kress. But as malls flourished and mega stores swallowed up many of these smaller retailers, consolidation reduced the number of diversified retail outlets. In the '70s and '80s, WHAM-O struggled to find retailers that would support products outside its Frisbee line.

Meanwhile, TV changed, too. In the 1960s, minute-long WHAM-O TV ads aired nationally on one of only three stations: ABC, CBS, or NBC. According to the National Cable & Telecommunications Association's Web site, "The 1984 Cable Act established a more favorable regulatory framework for the industry, stimulating investment in cable plant and programming on an unprecedented level." As the number of stations available to consumers grew, reaching those consumers with an affordable message about your hot, new, $1.00 toy became impossible. More expensive toys had to be created in order to justify the expense of marketing them via television.

In 1998, WHAM-O launched a successful line of food activity toys. Powered by licenses from Nestle, Kraft, and Baskin-Robbins, these contraptions sold well and were inspired by play gadgets like Hasbro's Easy-Bake Oven. The Jell-O Frozen Treat Maker, Baskin-Robbins Ice Cream Maker, Chuck E. Cheese's Pizza Factory, and Peep's Marshmallow Maker were some of the hits that WHAM-O designed before its success spawned copycats. With the category oversaturated, the company got out of the "food play" business. It didn't seem to fit anyway.

In 1999 the emphasis on outdoor fun returned with the reintroduction of Slip 'n Slide water slides. Today, the fun of Slip 'n Slide is strictly for kids, but it remains the biggest-selling WHAM-O item. The 2006 line consisted of twenty individual Slip 'n Slide products, ranging from a kids' car wash to heroic versions of the classic toy featuring Spider-Man, Superman, and Batman.

BELOW: This is not your grand-father's WHAM-O.

For many WHAM-O fans, its core sporting-goods products are synonymous with the beach. Frisbee, Hacky Sack, even Trac-Ball have all logged their share of time in the sand. And thanks to Kransco, the surf has not been without WHAM-O, either. According to Tom Morey's Web site, he invented Boogie boarding (or Bodyboarding) as ". . . an activity that, unlike surfing, offered a gentle learning curve and could be enjoyed immediately by even the most sedentary of people." Today WHAM-O continues to make a full line of Boogie boards and Bodyboards within its Morey and

Ages 5 & Up

WHAM-O® **SNOWMAN KIT**

Traditional

Have the coolest snowman on the block!

Durable weather p...

Reusabl... parts

Punk Rocker S... Kit sold sepa...

14 PIECE...

BZ brand divisions. WHAM-O strengthened its beach-fun dominance in 2003 when it added the Sea-Doo exclusive product license for inflatable fun on the sea.

Recognizing that its products were heavily weighted for summer play, WHAM-O diversified with Snow Boogie, a brand of winter fun in the form of sleds, saucers, snowboards, and toboggans. Add to this line some inflatable Ski-Doo snow discs and powderboards and a cool line of Snowman kits, and it's clear that WHAM-O wants to own the winter as well.

All these outdoor brands have made WHAM-O's call to action louder. In the hearts and minds of many, WHAM-O will forever be a company that encourages kids (and adults) to get outside and play. This is a very good thing. Maybe our current epidemic of childhood obesity would be calmed, if not cured, if parents would only encourage their kids to *get out and go*. According to the Centers for Disease Control and two National Health and Nutrition Examination Surveys, in the time period between 1976–1980 and 2003–2004, kids aged 6–11 years showed an increase in the prevalence of being overweight from 6.5 percent to 18.8 percent. Of course it's not just kids. Adults in the United States are equally at fault. We are the fattest nation on Earth, content to watch TV or get our play fix while seated on the couch, plugged in but tuned out. We are Americans Idle.

Yet WHAM-O stands at the forefront of companies able to foster change. At this writing a full-page ad is running in *Sports Illustrated* and other magazines, placed by the Department of Health & Human Services and the Ad Council. It encourages kids to "Get up and play an hour a day" while showing some kids jumping rope, playing Ring Around the Rosie, twirling hoops around their waists, and throwing a plastic disc. We don't know if those hoops are Hula Hoops or if that disc is a Frisbee disc, but everyone

knows what company popularized their play. Rich and Spud, the fishermen, hunters, campers, travelers, and *doers*, would be proud to have WHAM-O play a part in that initiative.

"I was so proud to come back to WHAM-O and see all those famous products again," Laura Sciutti said. Her tenure at Kransco ran from 1987 until it was sold to Mattel in 1997, but in 1999 she returned to WHAM-O when the company went back to its independent roots. "To see the Frisbees, the bodyboards, the Hacky Sacks—it's like coming home."

WHAM-O has returned home, too, celebrating its historic past with a 50th Anniversary Frisbee Set in 2007, while looking ahead to the company's future. Its new owner, Cornerstone Overseas Limited, has made a commitment to take WHAM-O global like never before. In a recent *San Francisco Chronicle* article, Jeff Hsieh, Cornerstone's chief executive officer, said, "This acquisition provides the Cornerstone group of companies the chance to leverage our worldwide manufacturing and distribution infrastructure with a classic and highly recognized brand name in outdoor recreation products dating back to the 1940s." Perhaps this is the key to WHAM-O's success, keeping one foot firmly grounded in classic outdoor sports fun, while striding forward to a future that finds Frisbee, Hula Hoop, Hacky Sack, SuperBall, and many more WHAM-O favorites in countries that have yet to discover them.

"One of the last things Spud really wanted was for someone to write a book about WHAM-O," Suzy Melin said. "He would be so honored. I know he would. I don't think in all his dreams he ever thought it would last sixty years." When asked if he ever dreamed his and Spud's little slingshot shop would last sixty years, Rich Knerr replied, "Has it been that long? Wow." The cofounder of the Fun Factory was speechless for a long time, his mind probably wandering through all the memories. When told that WHAM-O was planning a pretty big celebration for the anniversary, he was all at once a fresh-faced kid with a slingshot and a dream. "That sounds good," he said. "I think that would be fun."

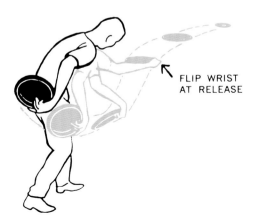

FLIP WRIST
AT RELEASE

Although every effort has been made to make this time line as accurate as possible, some posted dates are the result of logical guesses made with the best information available. As is the case with any toy company that has been bought and sold multiple times, much of WHAM-O's detailed history is sadly lost to time.

Thankfully, the new owners of WHAM-O recognize the company's legacy and the importance of rebuilding the company archives. Although this is not a complete listing of everything WHAM-O ever made, it is certainly the most comprehensive listing ever compiled.

Events are in bold; all other listings are WHAM-O products and their approximate release date. Products are alphabetized within their given year of introduction.

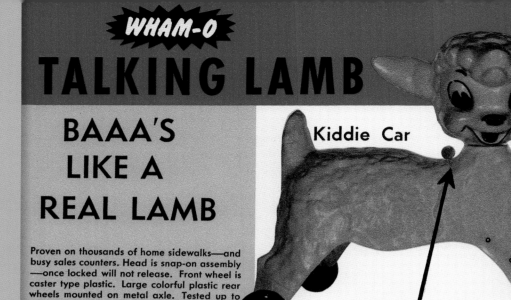

WHAM-O
TALKING LAMB

BAAA'S LIKE A REAL LAMB

Kiddie Car

Proven on thousands of home sidewalks—and busy sales counters. Head is snap-on assembly —once locked will not release. Front wheel is caster type plastic. Large colorful plastic rear wheels mounted on metal axle. Tested up to 200 lbs!

**LENGTH 23" - HEIGHT 18"
INDIVIDUALLY PACKED
WEIGHT 3¾ LBS.**

Just Pull
The Cord
Lamb Talks

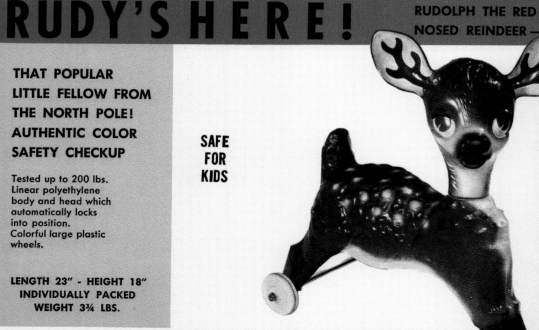

RUDY'S HERE!

RUDOLPH THE RED
NOSED REINDEER —

THAT POPULAR
LITTLE FELLOW FROM
THE NORTH POLE!
AUTHENTIC COLOR
SAFETY CHECKUP

SAFE
FOR
KIDS

Tested up to 200 lbs. Linear polyethylene body and head which automatically locks into position. Colorful large plastic wheels.

**LENGTH 23" - HEIGHT 18"
INDIVIDUALLY PACKED
WEIGHT 3¾ LBS.**

1948
Rich Knerr and Arthur "Spud" Melin form WHAM-O
The WHAM-O Slingshot

1955
Fred Morrison and his wife, Lu, design the Pluto Platter

1956
APACHE THROWING TOMAHAWK
BORNEO HUNTING BLOWGUN
DART GAME
JUNGLE MACHETE
SPORTSMAN HUNTING SLINGSHOT
TETHER BASEBALL TRAINER
THROWING DAGGER

1957
Fred Morrison licenses the Pluto Platter to WHAM-O
WHAM-O files for a design patent on the Pluto Platter
.177 BB PISTOL
DUELING SWORDS
HUF N' PUF SAFE BLOWGUN
JAI-ALAI
LAWN SHUFFLEBOARD
LARGE 6" MOON CAT (renamed PURPLE MOON CAT in 1958)
MR. HOOTIE (KITCHEN AND BAR TOOL)
PISTOL CROSSBOW
PLUTO PLATTER FLYING SAUCER
PLUTO PLATTER FLYING SAUCER HORSESHOE GAME
POOL GAME
POWERMASTER HUNTING CROSSBOW
RANGE TARGET
REGULATION TABLE TENNIS TABLE
SAILING SATELLITE
SMALL 3" MOON CAT
SNOWBALL GAME

1958
WHAM-O files for the trademark "Frisbee"
Fred Morrison is granted a design patent on his Pluto Platter
WHAM-O files for the trademark "Hula Hoop"
BALI-BALL (renamed WHING DING in 1959)
BOOMERANG
BOWLING BALL
CHAIN GANG COASTERS
DELUXE HOOP
GIANT HULA HOOP
GIANT TENNIS BIRD (renamed WHAM-IT in 1959)
HOME BOWLING SET
HULA BOARD
HULA HAT
HULA HOOP

LIL' HULA-HOOPEE
MALAYAN PISTOL BLOWGUN
MALAYAN RIFLE BLOWGUN
MEN'S EXERCISER
PISTOL CROSSBOW
PURPLE MOON CAT (renamed CUTE SCOOT in 1965)
PUSH-O-HOOP
SCOOT SHUFFLEBOARD
SKY BIRD
SMART BELLS AND SMART BELLES
SPUTNIK SAILING SATELLITE
TETHER GAME
WOMEN'S EXERCISER

—— 1959

CAP PISTOL
CIRCUS CYCLE
DRAW YARN
DUKE SNIDER (DODGER) BASEBALL TRAINER
FLING-A-RING
FUN FARM
GIANT AZTEC SUN CALENDAR
GIANT EASTER ISLAND HEADS
GIANT SOUTH SEA CLAM WATERFALL
GIANT TIDDLY WINKS
GOLFER'S PRACTICE BALL
KONTIKI IDOL
SPOON-BALL
TANK
TWIRL-A-PLATE
WACKY (BALLOON GAME)
WHAM-IT (renamed BIG BIRD in 1965)
WHAM-O AIR ROCKET WHING-DING
WHING-DING
X-15 SPACE PLANE

—— 1960

AQUA GLIDE WATER SKIS
CRICKET HOUSE
FUN-GUN (renamed AIR BLASTER in 1963)
KITTY KLEAN CAT PAN
MAGIC RECORD
POKER TABLE
SPEEDY SPINNER HULA HOOP
STAKE TABLE
TILT N' WHIRL
ZIPPO

—— 1961

LIMBO GAME
SLIP 'N SLIDE

WHAM-O Amazing New

CLIPPITY HORSE Fun!

NO DANGEROUS STICKS!

Just put it on--and ride away!

Leaves hands free to fight Indians

Safe, no stick to trip over

He's durable and doesn't eat much

COLORFUL
DUMP DISPLAY
NO. 260

SPECIFICATIONS		
Packed 2 doz. per carton		
Weight 8 lbs. 1½ oz. per carton		
Packed 4 doz. per carton		
Weight 15 lbs. 5½ oz. per carton		

© 1963 **WHAM-O** MFG. CO., 835 E. EL MONTE ST., SAN GABRIEL, CALIF. 91776

WHAM-O INSTANT BRICKMAKER

Compresses soft earth into hard building blocks!

WHAM-O TURBO-TUBE

PAT. PEND.

PRICE 98¢

AMAZING SPACE LIFT CHAMBER

FOR ANTI-GRAVITY **ACTION!**

FLIES LIKE MAGIC!

CIRCULAR WING — SPACE AGE, AERODYNAMIC DESIGN

STOCK No. 287

PLAY CATCH... FROM 20 to 200 FT.

(((GYRO-ACTION))) SPIN
FOR PRECISION-CONTROLLED FLIGHTS!

© 1966-WHAM-O MFG. CO., SAN GABRIEL, CALIF.

1966

Rich Knerr files for his patent on Zillion Bubbles
INSTANT BRICKMAKER
MINI SUPERBALLS
NUTTY KNOTTER
REGULAR MODEL FRISBEE
SMALL SUPERBALLS
SUPERBALL BASEBALL
SUPERBALL DICE
SUPERBALL GOLF
SUPER STUFF
TURBO-TUBE
WHEELIE-BAR

1967

Frisbee flying disc patent (pro model) awarded to Ed Headrick
International Frisbee Association is formed by Ed Headrick
Joel Silver and some high school buddies invent
Ultimate Frisbee
.12 CALIBER PISTOL
CAN PLINKER
DUCK-MATE DECOY
GIANT COMICS
HOTSPOT HEATER
MASTER TOURNAMENT MODEL FRISBEE
TOTALITE FLUORESCENT LIGHT
WILD WHIRLER (renamed SONIC HOWLER in 1969)
ZILLION BUBBLES

1968

FRISBEE MASTER MODEL
HAPPI HUT
SHRINK MACHINE
SUPER FOAM MACHINE
SUPER-LOOPER
WHIRLEE TWIRLEE
ZAP-A-BUBBLE
ZIP ZAP

1969

ART WEAR DRESS KIT
KOOKY FROOTS (TOY FRUIT-FLAVORED DRINK)
LIAR'S POKER
MOONLIGHTER PRO FRISBEE
ROCK-IT-TO-ME ROCKS
SILLY STRING
SONIC GYRO (THE HOWLER)
SUPER SWOOPER
FUN FOUNTAIN (DRINK MIXER)

URS OF COOL, WET, SLIPPERY, SLIDING

1999

Slip 'n Slide water slides return to the market for kids only

2001

E-SHOOP HULA HOOP
FRISBEE SPLASHER
FRISBEE TOSS
MAKE YOUR OWN HULA HOOP
SNOW BOOGIE
WIGGLIN' WATER SNAKES
WATER BLAST HOCKEY

2002

Arthur "Spud" Melin dies on June 28th at the age of 77
Ed Headrick dies on August 12th at the age of 78
WHAM-O buys BZ surf brands from Earth & Ocean Sports

2003

WHAM-O acquires Sea-Doo and Ski-Doo licenses
BACKYARD OBSTACLE COURSE
BATTLE SPY (SQUIRT GOGGLES)
BIRDIE GOLF
BUMPER GOLF
CREEPY GUMMI CREATION STATION
GLOW IN THE DARK AIR DARTS
PEEP'S MARSHMALLOW MAKER
SNOWMAN KIT
TRAP BALL

2006

WHAM-O, Inc. is bought by Cornerstone Overseas Investments
360 DEGREE AIR HOCKEY
DELUXE PINBALL SOCCER
GLOW ZONE NIGHT AIR HOCKEY
GLOW ZONE NIGHT AIR HOCKEY JR.
HOOP SLAM BASKETBALL
MEGA SHARK SLIP 'N SLIDE
SLIM LINE HOCKEY
SLIM LINE SOCCER

2007

50TH ANNIVERSARY FRISBEE DISC SET
FRISBEE INFINITY

2008

WHAM-O celebrates its 60th Anniversary
Richard Knerr dies on January 14th at the age of 82

Bibliography

BOOKS

Epstein, Dan. *20th Century Pop Culture.* New York: Carlton Books Limited, 1999.

Johnson, Stancil E.D. *Frisbee: Practitioner's Manual and Definitive Treatise.* New York: Workman Publishing Company, 1975.

Kaye, Marvin. *A Toy Is Born.* New York: Stein and Day, 1973.

Kennedy, Phil. *The Essential Guide to Collecting Flyin' Discs* (Published within *Flat Flip Flies Straight! True Origins of the Frisbee*). Wethersfield, CT: Wormhole Publishers, 2006.

Malafronte, Victor A. *The Complete Book of Frisbee.* Alameda, CA: American Trends Publishing Company, 1998.

Morrison, Fred, and Phil Kennedy. *Flat Flip Flies Straight! True Origins of the Frisbee.* Wethersfield, CT: Wormhole Publishers, 2006.

Skolnik, Peter L. *Fads: America's Crazes, Fevers & Fancies.* New York: Thomas Y. Crowell Company, 1972.

Sommer, Robin Langley. *"I Had One of Those": Toys of Our Generation.* New York: Crescent Books, 1992.

Stern, Jane, and Michael Stern. *Encyclopedia of Pop Culture.* New York: HarperPerennial, 1992.

Stern, Sydney, and Ted Schoenhaus. *Toyland: The High-stakes Game of the Toy Industry.* Chicago: Contemporary Books, Inc., 1990.

Van Dulken, Stephen. *Inventing the 20th Century: 100 Inventions That Shaped the World.* New York: New York University Press, 2000.

Wulffson, Don L. *Toys! Amazing Stories behind Some Great Inventions.* New York: Henry Holt and Company, 2000.

MAGAZINE, NEWSPAPER, AND INTERNET ARTICLES

Bush, Thomas, and Frederick Taylor. "Hoop Fad Slips Fast Despite New Efforts to Keep It Spinning." *Wall Street Journal*, October 28, 1958.

Emery, Dave. "Dad Idea on Popular Slip 'N Slide." *Long Beach Press-Telegram*, September 14, 1961.

Griswold, Wesley S. "Can You Invent a Million-dollar Fad?" *Popular Science*, January 1966.

Hamilton, John. "500,000 Hoops Going Round." *Melbourne Age*, July 4, 1967.

Joseph, James. "How Those Hula Hoops Go Rolling." *Mechanix Illustrated*, December 1958.

Kann, Peter R. "Fad-Fostering Firm Bounces Back with New Hit: Super Ball." *Wall Street Journal*, October 6, 1965.

King, Larry. "Art Linkletter Discusses His Career in Television." *Larry King Live*, CNN.com, June 30, 2000.

Mann, Arnold. "Preacher's Kid." *Time*, November 11, 2002.

O'Neal, Denise I. "Well-traveled Kessler at Home in Toy World." *Chicago Sun-Times*, February 17, 2006.

Raine, George. "Fad Factory Wham-O Finds Itself Back in Style." *San Francisco Chronicle*, May 6, 2001.

———. "Emeryville's Wham-O Sold." *San Francisco Chronicle*, January 20, 2006.

Sarkar, Pia. "John Bowes—Businessman and Art Collector." *San Francisco Chronicle*, October 28, 2005.

Staff Writer. "Whole Country Hoops It Up in a New Craze." *Life*, July 8, 1958.

———. "Flying Frisbees." *Sports Illustrated*, May 13, 1957.

———. "A Boom with a Bounce." *Life*, December 3, 1965.

Stoughton, Stephanie. "Virginia Beach Company Has a Small but Thriving Place in Toy Industry." *The Virginian-Pilot*, March 7, 1996.

Weiss, Joanna. "Toy Story." *Boston Globe*, August 21, 2005.

INTERVIEWS

Carrier, Mike (developer of Slip 'n Slide). Telephone interviews, September 19 and September 30, 2002.

Knerr, Lori (daughter of WHAM-O founder Rich Knerr). Telephone interviews, September 11 and September 17, 2007.

Knerr, Rich (founder of WHAM-O). Telephone interviews, September 20 and September 24, 2007; October 4, 2007.

Martinez, Jenny (former WHAM-O employee). Telephone interview, October 29, 2007.

Melin, Suzy, wife of WHAM-O founder, Spud Melin. Telephone interview, November 12, 2007.

Morrison, Fred (inventor of the Pluto Platter/ Frisbee, author). Telephone interview, November 1, 2007.

Roddick, Dan (former WHAM-O employee and multiple Frisbee disc champion). Telephone interview, October 31, 2007.

Sciutti, Laura (former WHAM-O employee). Telephone interview, November 1, 2007.

Stalberger, John (coinventor of Hacky Sack). Telephone interviews, August 15, 2001; October 8, 2007.

Stingley, Norm (inventor of SuperBall). Telephone interviews, September 6 and September 30, 2002; November 18, 2002.

Thompson, Devlin (collector). Telephone interview, October 5, 2007.

Tolmer, David (son of Hula Hoop developer Alex Tolmer). Telephone interviews, September 24, 2002; November 25, 2002.

Wehrli, Tom (Disc Dog competitor). Telephone interview, October 31, 2007.

WEB SITES

All Web sites were accessible at time of publication.

Author's blog: www.theplaymakers.com

Bubble-Thing: www.bubblething.com

BZ Pro Boards: www.bzproboards.com

Disc Dog: www.ufoworldcup.org; www.skyhoundz.com; www.k9frisbee.com

Footbag World: www.footbag.org

Freestyle Players Association: www.freestyledisc.org

Fred Morrison and Phil Kennedy's book site: www.flatflip.com

Frisbee: www.frisbeedisc.com

Hoop Fan Site: www.hooping.org

International Disc Dog Handlers Association: www.iddha.com

Morey Bodyboards: www.moreybodyboards.com

Professional Disc Golf Association: www.pdga.com

Roller Racer: www.masoncorporation.com

SuperBall Fan Site: www.superballs.com

Secret Fun Spot: www.secretfunspot.com/whamo

Tom Morey: www.tommorey.com/boogie

Ultimate Players Association: www.upa.org

United States Guts Players Association: www.gutsfrisbee.com

WHAM-O: www.wham-o.com

World Footbag Association: www.worldfootbag.com

NO SPECIAL SKILL REQUIRED

HOW TO DO A WHEELIE

TIM WALSH is an author, game inventor, and 18-year veteran of the toy industry. A frequent speaker on toys and games on radio and TV, he lives in Sarasota, Florida.